How to Start Trading in the Stock Market

Alan Newton

"Success occurs when opportunity meets preparation."
— Zig Ziglar

Introduction

It seems as though everyone is talking about the stock market. We hear many people saying that we should all be investing in the stock market so that we can make money and invest in our future. This all sounds good, but the problem is that with all of this advice to invest in the stock market, nobody seems to give advice on how to do that. It can be frustrating to want to start investing but not even know what the first step is.

Maybe you are not part of that first group of people. Perhaps you are not even aware of what the stock market is and why people are investing in it, let alone know how to go about it. There are many people who have heard of the stock market, but while it has piqued their interest, they have no idea what it's all about. Fortunately for both groups, this book starts with the fundamentals of stock investing so that you have a solid foundation of knowledge of the stock market and the options for investing in it.

The stock market is a great tool that anyone can use to invest in their futures and build their wealth. The great thing is that it is accessible to everyone. There was a time when only an elite few were able to invest in the stock market because it was not accessible to the average person, but that has changed in recent years. Now, anyone with a computer and a good internet connection can start investing. This helps everyday people to build the futures that they dream of through proper management of finances. The stock market creates more opportunities for the growth of your money than an average savings account. This means that you can increase your wealth at a much quicker pace than if you were just going to place it in a high yield savings account.

When we hear people talking about the stock market, it can seem like it is a very complicated topic. There are words and phrases that seasoned traders use that seem completely foreign to laypeople. While anyone can start investing in the stock market, you do need some sort of base knowledge to do it effectively. Just jumping in blindly is not a good strategy as you could end up losing money instead of gaining it. This is why I have written this book. I wanted to give those who want to learn about the stock market and how to invest in it the tools they need to get started.

There is a lot of information out there, so it can seem like an impossible task to figure out where to start. This book is going to start right at the beginning and move forward in a way that makes sense and is easily understandable. The elements that you learn will be built upon so that you can easily digest the information. By the time you come to the end of this book, you will not only know what the stock market is, but you will also be able to develop a strategy to do so that will best fit you and your goals. There is not just one way to invest in the stock market. There are plenty of strategies out there, and each one has its own pros and cons. You need to find the one that works for you, which is why simply following generic advice about the stock market doesn't work.

I have been investing in the stock market since I was 20. I am now in my mid-30s and have been making six to seven figures monthly for about a decade now. This has allowed me to live the life of my dreams. I travel the world whenever I want, and when I am not doing that, I "ball out" in my New York City apartment. It is the life that I have always wanted to live, and the right investments in the stock market have made it happen for me.

Since my very first investment, I have been experimenting with various strategies in the stock market. The stock market is one of my passions, and I take every opportunity to learn new ways of doing things that could generate a profit for me. I have been studying the stock market for about two decades now, and I want to be able to share that information. The life I live is not just reserved for me. Anyone can have it if they have the right strategies and information so that they can make the right decisions.

I have given advice to many friends and family members, and they have succeeded and have been able to improve their finances and are now closer to living the lives that they dream of. There are no selfish motives for writing this book, as I have nothing to gain from it. I have achieved many of my financial goals, and everyone else can too. I want to help you and all who read this book build financial security and wealth so that freedom and wealth are within reach.

If you have always wanted to learn about the stock market but have been confused about where to start, then you have come to the right place. I believe in building a great foundation so that all other information can be easily added to that. This helps with understanding and retaining what you will be learning. This is not simply an investment advice book. It is a book that will help you understand the system and then have the knowledge to develop your own investing strategy. Before we get into all the technical aspects of the stock market, let's start at the beginning by giving you a good knowledge base to build from.

Chapter 1: Know What You're Getting Yourself Into

If you want to start trading in the stock market, it is wise to understand it. Knowing what it is is the basis for everything else that you will learn about it. Most people just jump in without doing research or having a proper understanding of how the stock market works or even what it does. This isn't the best strategy when you want to get started with trading. So let's start with the basics and build from there.

What Is the Stock Market?

When you invest in the stock market, what you are actually doing is investing in individual companies. You put in money to purchase shares in a company. A share gives you partial ownership of the company. Now, this does not mean that you get to make decisions regarding the company. You actually have no say in what goes on in the company; you just own a part of it. Your stock makes up a very small portion of the company, and the majority shareholders are people who are involved in the company. There is a portion of the company that gets sold as shares to outsiders. This is what you can purchase on the stock market.

Each company has to list itself on the stock market so that investors have the opportunity to invest in them. The company gets broken up into many smaller pieces that allow multiple people to invest in it. A company has to be pretty well established to be listed on the stock market, so someone can't just start a company today and get on the stock market to get people to invest in it. Usually, companies are started and funded by private investors, and after it takes off and builds a solid reputation, it can be added to the stock market.

Once the company is listed on the stock market, it sells for a specific price. Each share has a specific value. An investor has the option to buy as many shares as there are available. They will also be able to sell their shares at any point. Once you buy a share, you are not tied to it forever and can buy and sell as you please. The prices of these shares will go up and down on a daily basis. This can be for a number of reasons. If the company has had a bad day in the press, its share prices can go down by a lot. Then the next day, there could be something else that happens that brings the stock price up. As more people buy shares in a company, its share price goes up. If lots of people start to sell their shares, the price goes down. It is all based on how people feel about the company on any given day.

History of the Stock Market

When people start talking about the stock market, it can seem like it is a really modern and complicated subject. While the stock market has developed a lot over recent years, it had its beginnings in the 1600s in western Europe. This was way before technology and corporations as we know them today.

The stock market or stock exchange—these two terms can be used interchangeably—is a digital or physical place where people can go and trade stocks in publicly traded companies. Now, the whole world can take part in the stock trade, but the process first started in Antwerp, which is in modern-day Belgium. It started there because Belgium was the center of international trade at the time. The Dutch East India Company was the first company on the stock market and was the only company traded publicly for quite a few years (SoFi, 2021).

Eventually, in the late 1700s, a small group of merchants got together and decided to create the Buttonwood Tree Agreement. This is where stock trading in the United States got its start. This agreement is what formed the basis of what is now the New York Stock Exchange. It was designed to create trust so that merchants and brokers could buy and sell with each other and have the public's best interest at the forefront. The men who created this agreement and were part of it would meet daily and trade their stocks and bonds with each other.

In the 1790s, the United States government wanted to push the development of financial sectors and westward expansion. This led to the creation of a stock exchange system to help them start the whole process, and that is when the Philadelphia Stock Exchange was born. There were no major changes in this area for quite some time until the early 1900s when Poor's Publishing started tracking 90 stocks on the market; this was the earliest version of the S&P 500. After the stock market crash in 1929, other stock exchanges started emerging; this was the start of the National Association of Securities Dealers Automated

Quotations (NASDAQ), which is still one of the top stock exchanges in the world. The stock market has had many other ups and downs. One of the worst stock market crashes happened in 2008, which I'm sure most of us remember as the housing crash that caused a massive recession (SoFi, 2021).

As you can see, trading shares in companies has been happening for quite some time. As the stock trade became an international market, people had to develop systems for fair trade as there were different currencies being used around the world. It is not like trading is a new idea; people have been doing it for years. However, it has never been as accessible or as easy to do as it is today. It started off with only a few select people being able to get involved, and now almost anyone who has the funds available to trade can take part in it. This is great for both the economy and for individuals who want to invest and earn money.

How Does it Work?

You already know that when you buy a stock, you are buying a portion of that company. Most companies have millions or even billions of shares on the stock market, which is why so many people can invest in the same company and buy multiple stocks in it. There are two main stock types: common stocks and preferred stocks. A common shareholder has voting rights and can attend annual general meetings and have a say in how the company conducts business depending on the percentage of stock they have. Some companies choose to have a class system in place so that the founders have more voting power and can control the bigger decisions. For example, Class A could have ten votes per share held and Class B would only have one vote per share held. Preferred stocks do not have voting rights; however, they do have preference to receive dividends and liquidated assets, should it be necessary (Hayes, 2020).

For a company to continue growing, it needs capital. When someone just starts up a company, they can get capital via loans or private investors. This should be enough to get the company off the ground and for it to start making money. As it grows, it will need more money than what a loan can provide. Also, a loan can be very risky and eventually cost the company lots of money with the interest that needs to be paid back. Listing the company on the stock market is the best way to raise capital.

In order for a company to be listed on a stock exchange, they have to meet certain criteria. These criteria are predetermined by the exchange. Criteria for listing could include being in operation for a certain amount of time or having proof of a certain amount of profitability. The stock exchanges are not regulated by any government. They are completely separate entities and fall under the category of self-regulatory organizations. These exchanges are designed to protect the investor through rules and regulations that they have set in place.

When someone lists their company on the stock market, they are putting parts of their company up for sale to the public. This allows anyone to buy into it and invest their money. This allows the firm to become a public firm instead of a private one whose shares are only held by a few people. Once people start trading shares, the price of them fluctuates depending on how valuable people think it is. The more valuable people think the company is, the more people will want to buy shares, and this will drive the price up.

You will be able to make a profit from stocks if you are able to sell them at a higher price than you bought them for. Professional traders are always researching up-and-coming companies that show promise. If you invest in a company when the stock price is low and then wait it out until it increases, you can sell your stocks and make a really good profit. This is how you make money through trading stocks.

In order to do any of this, you need to trade in the stock market. The stock market isn't just one place or entity—there are various stock markets all around the world. The two largest stock exchanges in the world are the New York Stock Exchange and Nasdaq. Through the exchanges, the current owners of shares can interact with potential buyers. It is important to note that the companies themselves do not sell you the shares. You are simply trading with other people who already have the shares in their possession. The companies rarely get involved in this process.

There are a number of ways you can set prices on the stock market. The most popular is by way of an auction. Buyers and sellers place bids and ask for offers until they get a price that they are happy with. Since there are millions of investors on a stock exchange, there will be varying opinions on how much a stock is worth. The stock exchange will match buyers and sellers up so that you don't have to go searching for people that are willing to pay the price that you want to sell for or vice versa. The average person would need a stockbroker who would play the middleman for the seller and the buyer. There are thousands of transactions that take place every minute and this causes constant fluctuations. There is no way that a stock would be the exact same price throughout the day. Once you have your stock, you can keep it for as long as you would like. Some people like to keep their stocks for a long time and ride out any low patches, while others react to market volatility and sell when they feel their investment is going down. This is the overall view of how the stock market works. It is not too difficult to understand, but this is just the surface level. There are lots of strategies and analytical approaches to trading in the stock market and doing a good job at it. All of this will be touched on in later chapters.

How Does it Generate Profit and Losses?

There are two ways in which an investor can make money from stocks. The first is dividends, and the second is capital appreciation. The way dividends work is that when the company makes a profit, it is distributed in cash to the investors. So if there is a company that has 1000 shares bought by investors and the company declares that it has made a $2000 profit, each share will get $2 of profit from that. The more shares a person holds, the more profit they would get. Capital appreciation relies on the worth of the stock itself. If the investor buys a stock for $5 and in a month, it is worth $8, they have made a $3 profit. The catch to this is that the profit is not a tangible profit unless the investor sells the stock for the new price. Since the stock market is volatile, if the investor waits a while, the price could drop or even increase. It is up to the investor to decide when the appropriate time to sell is. The wrong decision could mean that they don't make a good profit, or they could even sell at a loss.

Regardless of how you make money from a stock, there is always a risk to this. While predictions can be very good, they are never set in stone. It is important to note that there are no guarantees here. However, if you make smart decisions and use the right strategies, you will be able to make a lot of money from investing in the stock market. Sometimes taking a risk is what pays out the most. You could invest for a really low amount and end up cashing out a huge profit if you make the right choices. The reason there are so many people investing in the stock market is that it is a very profitable endeavor when you get it right.

Losses are also generated by the same principles. If you invest to get dividends and the company does not make a profit, you will not get a return. The money that you put in would have been lost because you did not get anything back. Even if the company makes a small amount of profit, it does not mean that you will gain profit from it.

The company would have to make a good amount of profit so that you get back more than you put in. When it comes to capital appreciation, there is no guarantee that the stock price will increase in value. Something might happen, and the company might do badly on the stock market. In this case, you have the option to pull out before you have to sell at too much of a loss, or you could wait it out and hope for the stock price to increase again.

The Up and Down Flow of the Market

The stock market is a complex place, and there are a lot of factors that could impact the prices of stocks in the market. It is not as clear-cut as company performance determining stock price. Two companies could be doing great and have the same profit margin in the same industry, but their stock prices could be completely different. If the market were efficient and ran on only the fundamental factors, the only things that would impact the price of a stock would be an earnings base and a valuation multiple. An earnings base would be something like the earnings per share (EPS). The EPS would show the stock owners' return on investment when they buy the stock. A valuation multiple would have two key factors: how much the stock is expected to grow and a discount rate, both of which would be used to work out the present value of the future earning stream (Harper, 2019).

Those fundamental factors may be important, but they are not the only things that impact the stock market and the price of the various stocks. In fact, the technical factors involved are more responsible for the up and down flow of the stock market than anything else is. There are lots of these technical factors at play at any given time, and they are usually a mix of external factors that impact the supply and demand for a specific stock. Let's go through some of the technical factors that could impact the stock price in the market.

Inflation and deflation can impact the prices of stocks in the market in many different ways. The direction in which inflation goes affects the valuations in the opposite manner. So if inflation is high, you will get a low valuation multiple and vice versa. Deflation is quite bad for the stock market in general, and you will most likely see a drop in the stock prices because there is a lack of confidence in pricing power. The strength of the economy of the company's market as well as the company's peers will also have an effect on stock prices. Sometimes it is not the company's fault when the stock price drops, but that of the whole sector. For example, if there is a big scandal in the cell phone industry and people start losing faith in the industry as a whole, the stock prices of Apple, Samsung, and others will go down even if they have nothing to do with the scandal and their product is still going strong. Investors can look at the peers of the company they are investing in and be put off the whole sector due to weakness being shown in certain parts of the sector.

Incidental transactions can affect the way the prices of stocks move. People can make insider transactions which are often pre-scheduled and can be driven by portfolio objectives. Large companies could also invest in a certain stock in order to hedge another investment, and this will affect the stock prices even though the investors may not believe that the stock they invested in has much intrinsic value. Since any purchasing of stocks can increase the demand for it, this will inevitably do the same.

Something that people would usually not think would affect the stock market is the demographics of the investors. People of different age categories invest or take their money out depending on their stages of life. Investors in their young adult years are usually trying to figure things out and are not investing large sums of money into stocks. We see that younger investors tend to just go with the trends and don't make too many bold or risky decisions, and they don't think too far ahead. This is often because they do not have the money to do so because they are just starting out in their careers and are trying to build themselves up.

Middle-aged people tend to be more involved in the stock market, and they funnel a lot of their funds into this type of investment. Since they usually earn more than their younger counterparts, they invest more money and buy more stocks. This is the age group that has the most impact on stocks: they can drive stock prices up because they can invest more. They can also cause stock prices to fall if they pull out because they can withdraw significant amounts of money. They are the most active and tend to make the most calculated decisions.

Older people start to pull their money out of their investments and sell their stocks. This is because once they reach retirement age, they want to enjoy their money, and they need it to sustain their lifestyles. Most people invest in their futures so that they will be able to retire and enjoy their retirement. We see a lot of people in this age group being risk-averse and not making too many new investments. They would rather settle for what they have and enjoy the money that they have accumulated.

Looking at these three groups, you can see that each one can have a different impact on the stock market. The thing is that some countries have a higher demographic of older people or younger people. If there are more people of retirement age that have invested in a stock, and they all decide to take out their money at around the same time, then the stock price will drop. A change could also happen if there are a lot of middle-aged people that enter the stock market and want to start investing. Demographics are not controllable, but it definitely impacts the stock market.

Trends and news also have a huge impact on the stock market. Sometimes a specific sector or stock is trending and people just jump on the bandwagon. This pushes the stock price up or down. You will also notice that if a prominent person expresses some sort of doubt in a certain stock, people just follow without doing their own research, and it drives the price down even though there is no solid proof that the stock is a bad investment. News also has a huge effect on the price of stocks. This is especially so with companies that are always in the spotlight. If something happens with a company—even if it has nothing to do with the value of the company or the profits—and it ends up on the news, the stock prices will reflect that. If, for example, a company is in the spotlight for not following environmentally conscious protocols, its stock price might decrease because there is negative news circling around it. These factors can also drive prices up if they create positive opinions.

This plays into market sentiment, which is another thing that could impact the price of stocks. The term refers to the psychology of those who invest in the market. A bad rumor or piece of news might cause the stock to stay at a low price even though all projections show growth and that the stock is a good investment. This is why the stock market does not move based on facts or figures. Movement is usually reflective of how people feel about a certain stock. It can be very heavily opinion-based even when all the evidence is pointing in the opposite direction. There is still a lot of research being done on market sentiment as it is pretty new in the field of behavioral finance. It is often subjective, obstinate, and biased, depending on the people who are influencing that particular stock.

As you can see, there are a lot of things that can influence the stock market and the prices of individual stocks. It is not as clear-cut as a company's price increasing simply because the company is doing well. There are a lot of different factors at play here. It would be easier to invest if you were able to tell how the flow of the stock market will go, but most of the time, it is really difficult to predict price fluctuations. There is always a chance that the stock market will take a turn that you don't expect. That is why it is important to be prepared and have the right strategies in place to deal with this.

How Do People Get Rich From Trading in the Stock Market?

This is the golden question. Most people who invest in the stock market do so to make money. There is not a person on earth who would willingly put their money into an opportunity and not want to get a good return on investment. You see people like Warren Buffet and other investors that have become millionaires and billionaires, and they all attribute it to investing in the stock market. It is definitely possible to make a good amount of money from the stock market, and it has been proven over and over again.

If you want to get rich through investing, you will have to have a long-term plan. Investing is not a get-rich-quick scheme, but it can set you up for the future you desire. The way you will be able to do this is by choosing a company that should be profitable and then holding the investment for the long term. Your investment should grow continuously, and you will be able to cash it out in the years to come. An investment portfolio should be built in a way that allows it to withstand any unforeseen circumstances.

While investing all your money into one stock is not the best plan, having one good investment can pay out major cash when the time is right. It is definitely better to diversify your portfolio so that if a few of your investments end up going south, you will still be able to reap rewards from the ones that succeed. We can never guarantee which ones will be lucrative in the end, but this strategy will give a better chance of investing in the right ones.

Many investors get scared when one of their investments starts taking a dive. Then they end up pulling out their money and selling the stock. The truth is that most stocks will take a downward turn at some point or another, but they also have periods of growth. If you sell prematurely, you end up giving away a great opportunity to get a good return on investment. If you hold, you have a better chance of seeing success in the end. Those that chop and change their investments all the time usually don't come out successful at the end.

What You Should Consider Before Getting Started

There are many things that come along with trading stocks. You should be aware of these before you start so that you go in with the right mindset. Often, people think it will just be a quick and easy process, only to find that they need to put in some work to see the results they want. You should consider the following three things before you jump into stock trading.

How Much Time Is Needed

Trading stocks takes time. You need to take time to learn how to do it properly, and then you need the time to actually do it. When I discussed the up and down flow of the market, I mentioned that there are two categories that could affect it. The first is the fundamental and technical factors that impact the prices of stocks in the market. The fundamental factors are very difficult to understand, and it would take a lot of studying and effort to learn how to predict the stock market using them. Technical factors, on the other hand, are much easier to understand, and they often take precedence over the fundamental factors. If you understand and are aware of the technical factors, you will be able to learn the stock market much quicker and will be able to make better decisions.

With fundamental analysis, you will need to learn how to understand charts and graphs that can be quite complicated. With technical analysis, you will just need to pick an indicator and make your decision based on that. It is a much more clear-cut approach and therefore is much better for beginners and those who do not want to overcomplicate the process. The only issue with this is that you need to pick the right indicator. Picking the right indicator can actually be an easy process if you just copy what other traders are doing. You will be able to follow their lead and not have to take a lot of time doing the analysis yourself.

You will also need to take some time to test out your trading strategy. This can take anywhere from one to three months. You can do this using a trading simulator. Testing is important to being successful at trading, those who are successful at trading usually always test first. This will give you a good idea of whether your strategy will work or not. This is time-consuming, but it is worth it in the end.

If you want to learn how to trade using technical analysis, it is not that hard, and it should take you a few days to learn it. However, it does take practice to get it right and become proficient in it. The more you practice, the better you will get at it, and practice does take time. You will probably make mistakes, but that's okay. You just have to learn from them and keep going. This is how you will become successful at trading stocks.

How to Stay Focused

If you are looking at day trading and being an active trader, you will need to remain focused throughout the process. Active trading involves watching the market and trying to beat it by buying and selling stocks strategically. This means that you have to be completely focused and limit the distractions around you. Any distraction could cause a lapse in judgment and cause you to make a mistake.

If you are going to sit down and start trading, you will need to carve out a portion of time to do this. Make sure that your phone is on silent and, if you live with others, that they know not to bother you at this time. The reason for this is that distractions can affect your emotions. Positive feelings might make you too optimistic, and Negative feelings might make you too pessimistic. Both of these can get in the way of making the right decisions.

The Best Time to Work

Trading and investing are two different things. When you invest, you aim for long-term goals, and you want to place your money somewhere it will grow without much involvement from you. Trading is an active process because the turnaround time is quite quick. With an active process, the question of what the best time to trade always arises.

The first thing you need to consider while trading is the opening and closing times of the market. The markets basically follow their local business hours, so the mornings can be quite wild for the stock market. This is because all the news and events that happened after closing time the previous day are causing some volatility in the market. If you are a beginner, it is best to avoid trading while the market is still very volatile. More experienced traders might be able to do it effectively as they have had some practice with it and can pick up on patterns. In fact, the first 15 minutes is prime time for more experienced traders.

The middle of the day is the best for beginners because the market quiets down and there are more stable movements. Beginners can trade without feeling pressure from market volatility, and it is a good time to practice. In the evening, the market becomes volatile again, and it is a good time for more experienced traders. Beginners should stop trading by this time otherwise they risk losing a lot of what they have earned.

Many believe that there is also an optimal time of the week and month to trade. There is not much evidence supporting this, however you should try it out and see if it works for you. Many traders say that Monday is the best day of the week to buy stock since it is just coming off the weekend and the best day to sell is Friday because people are more optimistic and positive. When it comes to the best time of the year, many people believe that the summer months and the turn of the year are the best times to trade. However, if you are a trader or looking to get into trading, it is not wise to only trade in certain months of the year. Consistent trading will not only help you get better at it, but it will also improve your returns.

When it comes to trading, you will technically never be off the clock. You need to understand that trading will be a 24/7 focus, and you will need to put a lot of effort into it. The market will fluctuate and change, and you should be ready for that. Of course, you will take breaks and aim to have balance in your life, but you should be ready to spend a lot of time on this and know that you should be consistent with the work you put in.

Managing Your Emotions

When people think about trading, they often don't think of it as an emotional task. However, emotions actually play a huge part in the trading process. You are going to have to deal with emotions such as hope, fear, and greed when you get involved in trading. If you make decisions that are motivated by emotion, you have a higher chance of making big mistakes that you will regret later. Keeping your emotions in check is crucial for being successful as a trader.

When you trade, you are playing a game of possibilities, and this can affect your emotions. You should detach yourself from the results of a trade. Otherwise, you will make your next decision based on that without even knowing it. If you have a good trade, you might be optimistic and hopeful and be a bit more reckless with the next trades. If you have a bad trade, you might be more pessimistic and not take the risks you need to.

It can be incredibly easy to get stuck behind the computer and just try to keep going the whole day. However, this is how you get caught up in emotions. You need to take a step back and remove yourself from the situation to clear your head. After each trade, take a walk. This way you get the opportunity to take your mind off trading, and no matter the outcome, you can detach yourself from the feelings involved with the trade before you get back to work. Another thing you should consider doing is stop trading for the day after three consecutive wins or losses. When you constantly win, you feel on top of the world and can make risky decisions. When you lose over and over again, you start revenge trading because you don't want to lose anymore and this can lead to bad decisions. Tomorrow is another day, so you can go again then. The other thing that you should not do is look at your profit or loss figure. This could impact you in the same way that multiple wins or losses can, so it is best to only look at it at the end of the day when you are done.

A Brief Overview of the Different Types of Trading

There are four different types of trading. These are scalping, day trading, swing trading and position trading. They all involve different things and take varying amounts of time and use different strategies. You can't expect every strategy to work for you, so you need to know what each entails in order to choose the best one for you.

Scalping and day trading are done in the short term. You will need to be quite involved in the process because stock prices change on a daily basis and even minute to minute. It involves strategy and commitment. Swing trading is more of a mid-term process as you will be working in terms of a few days and weeks. Lastly, position trading is a long-term type of trading. This can start creeping into the years as you might need to hold for a long time.

All of these have benefits, but they also have their downsides. It is important to pick the one that will work for you and that you think will give you the best return. I will be going more into details about the different types of trading in the next chapter.

Chapter 2: Focus On Strategies That Work for You

Every person is different, and that means that they will each need a different strategy when trading. The biggest mistake a novice trader could make is to choose a strategy just because someone they know is doing it. Different goals, personalities, and lifestyles mean that every person should take their own path and not copy what works for someone else. What works for someone else might be something that yields no returns or even negative returns for you.

The best trading strategy will be the one that excites you. Trading in the stock market is sometimes erroneously seen as a way to get rich quick, which is the reason that many new traders just copy someone else's strategy. This often leads to bad decisions and the person losing more money than they expected as well as wasting their time and energy. Understanding the types of stock trading as well as stock orders will help you to decide on a way forward that will be best for you.

13 Types of Stock Order

Once you have a stockbroker, you can begin trading. Before you get started on that process, you need to know the different types of trade orders and when to use them. You can place these orders online and while you will probably not use all of them, it is still good to know what is at your disposal.

When you buy stock, you are essentially placing an order. Someone else who is willing to sell it to you will come along. The type of stock order you engage in will change the way the process works. Some are more complicated than others, so it really depends on your preference and what you think will work best for you.

Market

The market is by far the most popular form of stock trade. When you trade on the market, you are essentially saying that you are willing to take whatever price is given to you. When you want to buy or sell, you transact with the price that is offered at the time of the offer. As soon as you place the order, it gets transmitted to the exchange, and you pay the current price of the stock. It is important to be aware that the market fluctuates quite quickly. So if the price of a stock is $100 when you place the order, you shouldn't be surprised if you end up paying a little more or less than that. It usually won't be too much, so you might end up paying $101.20 or $99.50. It isn't a big change, but it is still good to know so that you aren't taken aback when you place the order and end up paying more or less than expected.

Limit

A limit order is one that allows you to set an upper and lower limit to the price you are willing to pay or accept for a stock. You can set a maximum amount that you are willing to pay for the stock and a minimum limit for what you are willing to sell for. With market orders, it is almost a guarantee that the order will be fulfilled because you are just paying market price, but with a limit order, this is not the case. You do run the risk of not fulfilling the transaction if the price of the stock never falls within your limits.

Let's say there is a stock that you really want to purchase; however, you believe that it is overpriced at its current price. The price could be $85 per share, and you want to pay $80. You could set your limit at $80, and when the share price drops to that amount, the system will automatically purchase it for you. If the price never drops to that amount, it will not be purchased.

The other thing that you should be aware of when it comes to limit orders is that the limit that you have set is fixed. So if there is a very big drop in the share price, and it goes to $70, you will still pay the $80 because that is what your limit was set to. The system executes your order as soon as the share reaches your desired price. This is something to consider as you might end up overpaying if the price drops. The good thing about limit orders is that if the price drops to your limit and rises again, you get it for the lower price. So there are pros and cons to this type of order.

All-or-None

There might be a case when you want to purchase quite a large amount of a company's stock. Larger orders might take a while to fulfill because of their size, and you could end up paying different prices for each one. If you wanted to buy 100 shares in a company and there are only 80 available at the moment, the 80 would be confirmed and as the other 20 become available, the system will purchase them. This time in between allows the prices to increase or decrease.

If you wanted to pay the same price for all of the stocks, you would place an all-or-none order. This means that your order has to be fulfilled all at once or not at all. The only time it will be fulfilled is when there are enough shares available at once to match your order. You could end up waiting a while for this since you don't know when the right amount will be available. This order will stay in effect until you execute it or cancel it.

Fill-or-Kill

A fill-or-kill order is one that can never be partially executed. Once you put in this order, it will either be processed or it will be canceled. People use this if they want to place an order immediately and only want the stock at a specific price. They can place the order and if there are stocks for that price at the time they place the order, it is fulfilled. If there are no stocks for that price at the moment the order is placed, then it is rejected. The buyer can then go and place other offers for other stocks.

Immediate-or-Cancel

This kind of order works very similarly to the previous one. The biggest difference is that an immediate-or-cancel order can be partially fulfilled. When you place the order, the system accepts whatever is available at the price you set and once there are no more stocks at that price, the order stops and is canceled. You get to keep whatever was available, but your order may only be partially fulfilled.

Stop

This is a great tool that day traders use in order to lock in their profits. The stop order is set at a specific price. Once the stock reaches that price, the stop order turns into a regular market order. This means that the transactions go through and the normal rules apply. Your order is guaranteed but may have a different price from what you expect.

Stop Limit

A stop limit order automatically converts into a limit order once the stop price has been reached. You will set a price you are comfortable with, and as soon as the price reaches your amount, the transaction takes place. There is a chance that the transaction will not take place if the price never reaches your stop limit.

Short Sell Order

This type of order and the one mentioned after this go hand in hand. For a short sell order, you have to believe that a certain stock is overvalued. This must be a stock that you do not own. If you predict this correctly, and the stock falls to the price that it is actually worth, you will be able to profit from this.

Let's say that you think a stock is overvalued at the current price, which is $15. You can take advantage of this by selling borrowed shares of the stock at the overvalued price. Then you enter a short sell order for 500 shares of the stock and sell them on an open market. If you are right, and the price drops, you can use the next order type to make your profit.

Buy to Cover

This carries on from the short sell order. If you predict the price drop correctly, you can buy shares of the stock you shorted at a lower price to cover the borrowed shares you sold. If the price from the above example does drop to $12, you can place a buy to cover order so that you can complete the short sale order. The buy to cover order would purchase all 500 shares at $12 each and return the borrowed shares to the broker. Since you bought the shares for $3 less than they were sold for, you will profit the $3 per share, which would equate to $1500 in profit for you.

Day Order

With a day order, there is only a short amount of time in which the order can be fulfilled. If the order has not been fulfilled by the end of the business day, then it will be canceled. The end of the day is at 4:00 pm ET. This type of order is perfect for those who are not looking to extend the time frames of their order for fear of drastic price changes.

Good-til-Canceled

These types of orders remain open until they are canceled. They can be canceled either by being fulfilled, by your canceling the order, or by the time period determined by your broker having passed. It is easy to forget that these orders exist, and you may risk leaving them open for longer than intended. If you make one of these orders, you should keep checking on it and make sure that you cancel it at the best time for you if it isn't fulfilled.

Trailing Stop

This is a great option for those who want to automatically limit their potential losses while protecting any gains they might get from a stock. With this, you would have to set a stop price that is either a percentage of the market value or a spread in points.

Let's look at an example of this so that it is easier to understand. Let's say that you have just bought 100 shares in Dell when the price was $60 per share. The value is now $70 per share.

At this point, you want to make sure that you have at least a $7 profit per share even if the price drops for some reason. You also want to make sure that you will be able to make gains if the stock increases in value. You would put a $3 trailing stop on your order so that if the price were to drop, it would only drop to $67 before your money is taken out. This would still result in a $7 profit.

Now, if the value of the stock were to increase, your investment would continue to grow. If the value ends up being $80 per share at some point and then starts dropping, it will only be able to drop $3 before your shares are sold. In this case, you would sell your shares at $77 per share and make a $17 profit on each share. No matter how much the share price rises, your shares would be sold if the stock falls more than the $3 you set at the beginning. This ensures that you still get the benefits of the increasing prices and limit the amount of losses you face.

Bracketed Orders

This one works very similarly to the above order type. There is just one extra addition to it. Instead of just setting a lower limit, you can also set an upper limit. If the price of the stock goes up to a certain amount, the order will be stopped, and your stocks will be sold. If you take the above example with the lower limit set to a decrease of $3, you could now set an upper limit. Let's say you set the upper limit for $85 per share. Once the share price reaches $85, the order will be turned into a market order and be executed. The lower limit would still apply, so you have set boundaries on both sides.

Day Trading

Day trading can be quite rewarding if the right strategy is implemented. Those that go in with no strategy often end up losing a lot of money and making some bad decisions. This means that day trading can be quite challenging for beginners because it can be quite technical in the way that you trade. If you are thinking about getting into day trading, then you need to take some time beforehand to create a good strategy that will actually lead to success.

When I say day trading, I'm referring to the process of buying and selling a security within the span of a single trading day. In order to get into day trading, it is best to have a lot of funds at your disposal. This is because day traders use high amounts of leverage to capitalize on small changes in price. Most day traders do so in the stock market or in the foreign exchange market. These two platforms offer the most change in price in the short term and that is the optimal environment for day traders to get the best returns (Kuepper, 2021).

In order to day trade successfully, you need to keep up with what is going on in the news as this impacts short-term price movements in the markets. Many people hop into day trading because they believe that they can make a lot of money in a short amount of time. However, if you do not have the right knowledge and understand what is going on in the market, you will not be able to gain profits from it. Day trading does take work and planning, so it is definitely not wise to just jump in and throw all your money at it without any background information to back up your decisions.

Most professional financial advisors and money managers do not take part in day trading because they believe that the reward is not worth the risk involved. This is not to say that it is impossible to make money using day trading. It is just that the success rate is lower than those of long-term strategies. The reason for this is that day trading can be quite complicated and there is a higher amount of risk involved.

There also tends to be more scams involved with day trading because people are looking for a way to get rich quickly. Scammers take advantage of this, and this can result in the day trader losing their money.

Day trading is not for everyone, but there are those that really make a success of it. If you have the time and resources to put into it, then there is no reason you shouldn't try. You should have knowledge of the market and the product you are choosing to trade. You will also need to have a good amount of capital to place into the market. The key is only using money you can afford to lose. Putting all your money into a day trading market is not a good strategy. At the end of the day, trading can be unpredictable, so it is not wise to bet it all on the market. Once you have decided to get into the day trading market, you must stay true to the strategy you have set for yourself. Making decisions based on emotions never actually works out. Using a trailing stop loss is actually an excellent strategy for day trading as it can minimize your losses while still protecting any gains you have made.

Pros and Cons

As with everything in life, there are pros and cons to day trading. Understanding what they are will help you make better decisions and decide whether this is the best trading strategy for you.

One of the biggest pros is that you see instant results from day trading. With most other trading strategies, it can take a while before you start to make gains with them. Day trading offers results on the day you are trading. This leads into the second pro, which is that there is no overnight risk. When you day trade, you only work during the day, and once the stock market closes, so do you. All of your money will be out of the market, so whatever happens during the night will not affect you. A lot can happen overnight that can cause a huge swing in market prices.

Another advantage, and the reason so many people actually like day trading, is that it gives you an adrenaline rush. You have the opportunity to double, triple, or even quadruple your initial investment in just a matter of hours or even minutes. That is definitely exciting. There is no denying that this feeling can be addictive, so if you find yourself getting too caught up in the emotion of it all, it is wise to take a step back.

The final pro is that this type of trading does not allow for overthinking. Many people make bad decisions because they overthink. There is no time for that with day trading.

Next let's move onto the cons, the first of which is that it may require quite a large amount of starting capital. In some cases, the amount required is $25,000. This is to protect investors who are less wealthy from losing too much from risky trading. If this is a problem for you, then day trading stocks may not be the best option for you.

Another con to consider is that because you are only working within the space of a day, your stop may be smaller and that can result in smaller profits. There is only so much a price can move within a day, and for the most part, this number is not large, so you should expect that the profit you make per day might be quite small.

Not being able to think clearly and overtrading are also cons when it comes to day trading. While one of the pros of day trading is that you can't overthink, the flip side of the coin is that you don't have time to think. With day trading, you are usually making snap decisions rather than taking a few minutes to think things through before placing an order. This can lead to some bad decisions that you might regret as soon as you make them. Moving on to overtrading, which is the practice of trying to make up for a bad day by continuing to trade. Bad days are inevitable. There will be some points where things will not work out for you. This is the point people try to convince themselves that if they trade more, they will be able to make up for all that they have lost. Usually this does not work because you will be making trading decisions based on emotions. This is something that many day traders fall into, so if you find that you are losing money continuously, it is best to take a step back and come back the next day.

Swing Trading

When someone takes part in swing trading, they are aiming to get short to medium term gains in the stock market. This means that they will be trading over a period of a couple of days to a few weeks. The time frame can be extended to a few months and still be considered swing trading. When you swing trade, you hold your position for more than one session. The goal of this type of trading is to capitalize on the chance of a potential upward price movement. Traders can go either for volatile stocks that have a lot of movement or for ones that are more sedentary and move slowly. Whichever strategy they choose, the goal is to pick the stock that has the most potential to move in a favorable direction.

A successful swing trader is only looking to get a good chunk of the price move and is then ready to move on to the next opportunity. Since this is a short- to medium-term trading situation, most traders choose where they are going to put their money based on technical analysis. Fundamental analysis can have its place here to make sure that the trends are in your favor, but it does not play a major role in deciding which stock to pick. Looking at daily charts as well as hourly and 15 minute charts may be helpful because they will give insight on when the best time to enter the market is.

Pros and Cons

The first pro is that swing trading does not have a huge time commitment. While it definitely takes up more time than long-term investing does, swing trading requires a much shorter time commitment than day trading. If you check your stock and do the analysis once a day, you should be fine. This also allows you to trade part-time, which is another point in favor of swing trading. Since you only have to be involved once a day, it does free you up, so you can focus on other areas of your life.

The other pro here is that you can actually make a good amount of money when you swing trade. This is with a good strategy and consistency. If you are not consistent and don't make sure to keep an eye on your stocks, then your trades might not be as profitable as you hoped. Consistency is key.

On the other hand, the cons of swing trading include exposure to overnight and weekend gaps. Unlike with day trading, which has no risk of overnight downturn, with swing trading there is that risk. These gaps can cause a trader's stop loss to be useless, so this is something to consider. Another con is that you might miss out on potentially good stocks because you pulled back too soon. With swing trading, you will be trying to take advantage of price swings. You will try to get in right at the beginning and then pull out when you believe that the price is going to start dropping again. Since stocks can be unpredictable, this may not happen and the price of the stock could continue to increase, and you will have missed out on that additional profit.

Another con to be aware of is that it is quite difficult to time the market. You can do all the research you can, but sometimes the result will be the complete opposite of what you thought it would be. You also have to consider the trading costs as you will be paying a fee every time you enter the market. The cost will definitely be lower than that of day trading, but it is still something you would need to consider before jumping in.

Investing

Investing is a long hold strategy. You have probably heard people say that they are investing in the stock market. What this means is that they have picked a few stocks that they think will be profitable and have bought shares in those companies. Usually these investors leave the stock market to do its thing and are not looking to sell their shares any time soon. They will usually ride out the dips in price if they believe that the share price will pick up again. The strategy is the longer you can hold the stock, the more you will be able to make in the long run.

When you invest, you should not expect to see returns in the near future. Investors can leave their shares to grow for several years before they decide to sell for a profit. The people who invested in Apple in 2010 Can really reap the rewards of holding on to their shares since the price per share has doubled many times over. The secret to investing is to pick a stock that will increase massively in the future. You have to be able to see which companies have potential so that you can get in there early. You also have to have the courage to ride out the dips in prices, which will undoubtedly happen. The nature of the stock market is that it goes up and down. Investors look at an overall upward movement instead of what the stock is doing in the short term.

Investing is definitely far less work and much less time-consuming than day trading and swing trading. You will have to do your initial research and once you have made your investment choices, you can just let the stock market do its thing and take the price up to where you would hope it will be. You will also have the freedom to sell your stocks if you see that your investment is performing badly. It is wise to still keep your eye on the market while you are investing so that you are aware of any downward trends that may result in your losing money.

Pros and Cons

One of the best pros of investing is the opportunity to grow with the economy. As the economy grows and expands, so do the earnings of corporations. This means that the more jobs are created, and the more income is created, the more your investment can grow. It is also the best way to stay in front of any inflation. Unfortunately, inflation is a reality, and we will all face it a few times in our lives. Keeping money in a savings account is not going to help you when inflation hits. This is because the value of your money will decrease because your interest rate on the savings account may not exceed the rate of inflation. When you invest in the stock market, you can expect to get an annualized return of about 10%, which is more than the annualized inflation rate. You will have to be able to buy and hold even when the value drops so that you can reap the rewards when the value jumps back up.

Another plus to investing in stocks is that it can provide you with two income streams. You will make gains when the stocks you own increase in value, and you will be able to earn dividends from the profits of the companies that you have invested in. Not all companies offer dividends, so you will have to look for ones that do and then invest in them in order to get this benefit. Dividends are not available for day and swing traders.

Let's look at the cons of investing, of which the first one is that it takes a long time for you to be able to actually have more money to spend. When you invest, you are playing the long game, which means that you are putting your money into the stock market for future benefit. You probably won't have the spendable with you for a very long time because you are allowing your assets to grow in the market.

You could also make emotional decisions in the short term that could result in your losing money. It can be difficult to watch your stock go down in price and still hold and hope for it to come back up. The stock price may never go back up to the amount that it was, and that means that you will be selling at a loss. This is why when you are investing, you should always have a well-diversified portfolio so that if this does happen, you still have other stocks that are making you money. You will also have to keep abreast with what is happening in the stock market and with companies. It can be a lot of work to keep researching and finding out whether your investments will stand the test of time. You should not worry too much about small things in the news, but bigger things are worth paying attention to. You will be in a better position if you research constantly and make sure that you are in the know about what is going on in the market.

Options Trading

An option is also known as a stock option or an equity option. It is essentially a contract between the seller and the buyer. This contract concerns the stock or any other investment that is being purchased. It gives the buyer the power to enforce whatever has been specified in the contract within a specified time frame. This might seem a bit confusing, but let me explain it using an example. If there is a call option on the stock that states that the buyer is entitled to buy a set number of shares at a predetermined price, the option seller must sell the stock at the predetermined price if the buyer exercises the option. The buyer has the option of whether they would like to use the option. This is where the name comes from.

Option trading gives the buyer the power to choose whether they want to follow the specified rules or not. This means that the buyer can choose to exercise the option when it works for them, but if it doesn't, they are under no obligation to do so. To further clarify the above example, let's say that a certain call option has a stock for $70, but the market price for that same stock is $40. The buyer should not buy it from the option holder as they can get it for much cheaper on the open market. However, if the stock is trading for $80 on the open market, it would be smart for the buyer to use the option because they would be purchasing it below market value.

Pros and Cons

There are quite a few pros to options trading, so they must be considered when deciding whether you want to go into it or not. As an investor, you have more exposure to cheaper options that will allow you to get into the market at a lower price. This is something that a lot of other traders will not be able to do. This will allow you to increase your profit margin. It can also reduce the risk of your portfolio in general, since it protects you from any potential drops in prices since you entered the market at a low price point.

The earning potential is also higher because of the way option trading is set up. There is also room for more strategy since there are many methods and types of options trading. It can be quite lucrative if you take the time to do your research and develop a strategy that will result in the best returns.

The first con to options trading is that there is less liquidity than with normal trading. This means that the trader can't jump in and out of the market as quickly as they can with other forms of trading. The fees are also higher with this type of trading, so it might end up costing you more to get involved. There are some brokers that offer discounts, but you would have to search for them and do your research to make sure that they are legitimate.

One of the biggest cons to options trading is the time decay. The value of your option could go down quite a bit regardless of the underlying value of the stock. The option market can be more volatile than the regular stock market and this often shocks those who come from other forms of trading. Another thing you should be aware of is that you can't just jump into options trading. There are often other requirements that need to be met in order for you to use options as part of your trading strategy. You will probably have to read some educational material on it so that you are aware of how it works and all the intricacies of it. This is a lot more initial work than with other forms of trading.

Trading on Margin

Trading on margin is a strategy by which the buyer only pays a percentage of the amount needed to purchase the stock. The buyer then borrows the rest of the money from the brokerage firm. In this case, the broker acts as the lender so that the buyer is able to purchase the stocks they want to. In order to buy on margin, you will need a margin account, not just a normal brokerage account.

In essence, this is a loan offered to the investor so that they can purchase assets with money they do not currently have in their account. There is interest that needs to be paid back to the brokerage for using the margin, and that means that any profits are lessened, and losses are magnified. This can be incredibly profitable if the investor earns more than the interest that accrues.

Every investor who wants to trade on margin will have a certain margin requirement. If your margin requirement is 70%, that means you would need 70% of the total amount of the stocks you want to purchase. If you want to purchase $10000 worth of stocks, then your margin requirement would be $7000. If you have that amount, you can then borrow the rest from the broker. You will not be able to borrow the total amount needed for the purchase of the stocks. You will also need an initial investment of $2000 if you want to open a margin account. This is called the initial margin, and from there you will be allowed to borrow up to 50% of the total price of the stock. You do not have to borrow the full 50%. In fact, it is usually better to borrow as little as possible so that your interest is not too high. Each brokerage will also have its own terms and conditions surrounding margin accounts, so make sure that you understand them fully before committing (Fernando, 2019).

You have the option to keep the loan for as long as you would like, but you must fulfill the terms in your contract. These terms usually include making your interest payments on time. There might be other stipulations, so it is best to thoroughly read through your agreement before you open the account. When it is time to sell the stock, the proceeds will first go to the broker to pay off the loan, and then you will be able to keep the rest. You also have to have a maintenance margin, which is the minimum amount of money you must have in your account. If you do not have this, your broker will force you to deposit more to make up this margin, or they might sell some of your stocks in order to funnel the money into the account. Neither of these is ideal, so it is best to know what your maintenance margin is and make sure that there is always enough in the account.

Pros and Cons

The greatest pro and the main reason people choose to open up margin accounts is that it boosts your purchasing power. This is very helpful when you have a small amount of money to invest but want to make some substantial purchases. If used carefully, it could easily boost your returns and diversify your portfolio. You will also increase your options with the margin account because you will have more money to play with. When you have a margin account, you have more options as to what you can do with your account, and you are not just stuck to the basic strategies of trading. You can even bet against stocks or dip your toes into various other stock option strategies. Of course, this can be more risky than the traditional way of buying stocks, but it creates more ways for the investor to make money.

While there are some great advantages to buying on margin, you have probably figured that it comes with its risks. One of the biggest risks you will be taking here is that you really cannot guarantee that the stock you have chosen will perform the way you think it will. Even the most experienced traders will get it wrong a lot of the time, so this is definitely a risk you will need to consider. If the initial value of your investment goes down, then you would be expected to cover the shortfall by adding more money into your margin account to cover it. This means that if the investment declines in the market, you might end up losing more money than you would have if you had bought the stocks using a regular trading account.

The other thing to be aware of is that the broker will only be concerned about protecting their loan. So if your accounts fall below the required amount, they will not think twice about liquidating some of your investments in order to make up the amount that they need in the account. They will usually give you a week or so to add more money to the account to bring the margin up, but after that, they will do what they have to do to protect the loan they have given you so that they do not lose out in the end.

Another downside to a margin account is that you will owe interest to the broker. It basically works just as a loan from the bank does. You would need to make sure that your investment growth exceeds the interest you are paying, otherwise it would not be worth it. If you are paying 8% interest, then your investment growth should be around 10% or more because if it is 8%, you would end up breaking even, and that's not really worth it either.

Short Stocks

The process of short stocks has already been explained in the previous section about short sell orders. This is a very advanced trading strategy, so it should only be adopted by experienced traders. As a beginner, it is good to know about this strategy so that you might be able to use it at some point in the future, but it is not advisable to jump right into this kind of trading.

In short selling, the investor is trying to make a profit from the borrowed shares before they have to hand them back to the broker or dealer. The investor would also need to open up a margin account to participate in short selling. The regular rules for a margin account would apply here, so this is just an add-on to that. If you are interested in short selling, you should take into account the interest rate on your account as well as any fees you would incur throughout the process. You should also be aware that if the price increases the investor would lose their money and there is actually no limit to this increase because the share price could potentially increase indefinitely (Hayes, 2021).

Pros and Cons

The most obvious pro when it comes to short selling is that the investor can make a large profit when the stock goes down. There isn't any other strategy that offers this kind of return because everything else hinges on the stock improving in performance. It definitely adds another layer to stock trading, and many investors who have been in the game for a long time are excited by this opportunity.

The other advantage is that you will be able to hedge your portfolio. This is a great asset to have if something goes wrong in the market, and we hit a financial crisis. You could use your short selling portfolio to offset any losses you have incurred in your other trading portfolios.

The biggest risk is that you could face unlimited losses. This does not happen all the time, but if you have picked a good stock that actually increases in price, this could continue indefinitely. This means that you would be sitting at a loss since you would have to buy the stock back at a higher price than you sold it for. Another thing to consider is that you do not get paid dividends from these kinds of stocks. The reason for this is that the broker you borrowed the stocks from is the one who can earn the dividends from it. Remember, you don't actually own the stock, you are just borrowing it for the time being and will eventually have to give it back.

The other thing you need to consider is that you would need to have an open and functioning margin account. This means that short selling is not something that you can easily begin doing, especially if you don't have much capital to begin with. You would have to meet all the aforementioned requirements in order to take part in it. It might seem simple on paper, but once you get into it and realize all the little things that are involved, you will quickly see that it is not an easy process to jump into. As a beginner, it is better to just focus on the other areas of trading until you have more experience.

Final Thoughts on Trading Strategies

There is quite a lot of information to digest in this chapter. As you can see, there are a lot of ways in which you can trade and each one has its own benefits and downsides. It is good to take some time to sit down and weigh your options before you decide on which one you want to go with. There is a good chance that you felt a calling or a pull toward one or two styles of trading. These are the ones you should do more research on as they are the ones that resonate most with you and probably fit your lifestyle better.

While you might have a good idea of where you want to start trading, it is important to not jump the gun on this. There is a lot of other information to go through in this book that will help guide you along your journey. It is better to have a broader perspective than it is to just jump in because you feel a calling to one type of trading. Building a solid foundation is important so that you don't end up making big mistakes down the road.

Chapter 3: Become the Most Educated One in the Room

Learning all you need to before getting started is the best thing you can do to set yourself up for success. Many beginners just jump into trading and investing out of pure excitement because they think that it will be an easy process. This is not a good strategy as you could end up making some bad decisions. If you really focus on gaining knowledge at the beginning, you will be thankful when it comes time to dive into the world of trading.

The reason you should have a good foundation of knowledge is that it will prevent you from learning lessons the hard way. You will definitely make mistakes along the way, but there is no reason for you to make the same mistakes as other people when it is avoidable. Lessening the number of mistakes you will be making will accelerate your growth and make you more successful in the long run.

There are many other people who have gone on the same journey as you, so why not learn from them? Trust and analyze other people's testimonials and experiences so that you don't have to go through those negative situations. Understand the red flags that have popped up on their journeys and try to recognize those same red flags when you are trading.

Patience Is Key

When it comes to investing in the stock market, the most important thing is that you remain patient. In today's world, there is not a lot of emphasis on being patient because everyone wants things done instantly. When you don't take the time to pause and think about your actions, you have a higher chance of making emotional decisions that could result in big mistakes. Patience is actually one of the most important principles of investing, and it is very much overlooked.

There are many out there who think the most important thing in investing is timing the market. This is why they look at stats and charts trying to figure out the perfect time to invest and then cash out. However, this is not the most effective way to invest your money. Investing in the long term and holding your investment is one of the best strategies for overall success. The key is to start investing early and then being patient while your money grows and works for you.

You also don't have to invest a lot of money to reap the rewards of investing. The important thing is that you invest what you have and then leave it for as long as possible. The principle of compound interest will work in your favor, which is why time and patience is more important than anything else when it comes to investing your money. The importance of patience applies to both market compounding and investing in individual stocks. Even someone as experienced as Warren Buffet likes to hold on to certain stocks for the long term so that he can get the most out of it. Companies can grow exponentially and this means that you will benefit from waiting to sell. If you are able to pick the right stocks, the long game will work better than jumping from stock to stock.

Being Educated Before Trading Is Important

Having knowledge beforehand is very important for many reasons. One of the reasons is that you will be able to expose yourself to different strategies and methods of trading. If you go with the first strategy you hear of, you will be very limited. Not everything will work for everyone, so you need to expose yourself to as many avenues of trading as possible in order to find the one that best suits you.

Being educated in the world of trading is actually a continuous process, but it is also a habit that needs to be built before you jump in. There will always be something new to learn about and to improve on. There will always be new trends and news that you will have to stay up-to-date with. If you have already gotten into the habit of gathering information and learning, it will be easy to continue doing this into the future.

You will also be able to develop your own plan and strategy when you have fully educated yourself. You will be able to analyze and think about what will be the best move for you. There really isn't one cookie cutter approach to trading, so you will have to make the decisions on your own. You will be able to match up your goals with the right strategy to reach them.

This all leads you to the question, "How do I educate myself?" Well, you are already doing that by reading this book. However, it should not stop here. You will need to continuously seek more information. This does not mean that you have to take expensive classes. Books, blogs, and even YouTube can be great sources of information. Books tend to be safer as they have been vetted and can give you a good amount of knowledge in the pages. When it comes to blogs and YouTube videos, it is best to listen to people who have a proven track record in the field. There will be many people out there who have opinions, and some of them may even be successful in the short term, but you never know what will happen later on down the line. Listen to people who have been trading in the stock market for a long time and who have tried out a variety of strategies. These are the people who will give you the most sound advice.

You should also be looking for a mentor. If you can find someone you already know who will be able to help you and guide you, that is an amazing option. However, most people might not have such a person in their lives, so you can also get an online mentor. Someone can mentor you without you ever meeting. People like Jim Cramer and Warren Buffet have a whole host of information and advice online that you can learn from. They can be your mentors even though they will probably never know you exist. The important thing is that you are choosing people with experience and sound judgment to help guide you.

What You Should Know Before You Get Started

There are a few things that you should know before you actually get started with trading. One of these things is that you can set up a demo account to practice trading and get the hang of it without risking your money. This is one of the greatest tools available to the novice investor. You will be able to practice your strategies as well, so this is not just good for beginners who are finding their feet. Take advantage of demo accounts so that you can learn and practice before you have to jump into the ring with the real traders.

Another thing that you should take note of is that you will need some equipment to get started. This is nothing too complicated, but the better quality equipment you have, the better. Firstly, you will need a good computer—it can be a desktop or laptop. It should be able to run your trading program without lagging or crashing, so make sure you have a good processing speed. You don't want to miss out on good trading opportunities because your computer has frozen in the middle of the action. Having a second screen will also make you more efficient, although it is not completely necessary. You can always save up and buy one later on down the line.

You should also have a fast and reliable internet connection. This is especially important if you are day trading as it requires quick actions. If your internet connection is slow or spotty, it will get in the way of your performing successful transactions. Look for a reliable service provider that has a good reputation in your area. Once you have a good computer and internet connection, you can start looking for a broker. This is someone who facilitates your trades and charges a commission fee in exchange. You want someone who is reliable and who will be able to provide you with timely support, so sometimes the cheapest option is not the best one. However, the fee does play a big part in the decision-making process, especially if you are a day trader. High fees will cut into your profit. Do your research and pick a reliable broker.

Jargon You Should Understand

Once you start trading, or even just researching, you will find that there are a lot of terms traders use that are not used in everyday life. This can cause some confusion and make the whole process seem much more complicated than it actually is. This can also lead to you feeling demotivated if you are not able to comprehend what is going on.

Don't worry, I've got you covered. There is a lot of jargon that is used in the world of stock trading. It would take another book on its own to go through every single bit of terminology, so I will be going through the most important ones and the ones that you will definitely come across in your stock trading journey. These are the ones that will help you properly understand concepts and what is going on in general. So here they are, along with their definitions:

Ask - A certain price that a trader offers to sell their stock for.

Bid-Ask Spread - The gap between the lowest price someone is willing to sell, and the highest price someone is willing to buy a share for.

Bull Market - A market in which the stock prices are continuously rising.

Bear Market - A market in which the stick prices are continuously falling.

Volatility - The statistical measure of how quickly the stock market moves up and down.

Liquidity - A stock's ability to be bought and sold fairly quickly. The quicker the stocks can be bought and sold, the more liquid they will be.

Trading Volume - The total number of stocks being bought and sold at a specific time.

Market Capitalization - The total value of all the company's shares. This is also known as market cap.

IPO - Initial public offering, which refers to the first time a company sells its shares on the stock market.

Blue-Chip Stock - Large, well-known companies that have probably been in the stock market for a long time. They usually pay dividends and offer profitable increases.

Hedge Fund - An investment fund that can use investment and stock trading techniques that are not standard.

Mutual Fund - A pool of money paid by investors that is then invested in stocks, bonds, and other assets.

Stock Portfolio - An investor's collection of stocks.

Stock Broker - A person who buys and sells stocks on behalf of investors. In exchange, the investor pays them a fee, which is commonly a percentage based on the profits of the investment.

Pink Sheet Stocks - Stocks you can purchase for $5 or less, also known as penny stocks. You can purchase them over the counter, and they are not found on any of the big stock exchanges. Pink sheet stocks are usually just smaller companies.

Yield - The percentage of return on investment from the payment of a dividend.

Additional Resources

The most important thing that you can do for yourself in the world of investing is to continuously learn. The more you learn, the better you will be and the better returns you will see. There will never be a point where you will know everything. While this book is great and highly informative, there is no way that I can cover everything. This is why I have put together a list of other resources that you can dive into.

Everyone has a different learning style, so some methods will be better for certain people. You need to find out what works the best for you and figure out how you enjoy learning. I would suggest trying out a lot of different learning styles and types of information before you decide on what helps you the most.

Books

Books are one of the best ways to learn. There is a wealth of knowledge in them, and you can glean information from people who are very experienced in the field. Books are also not that expensive, so you don't have to spend a ton of money on getting educated. There is a reason that many extremely successful entrepreneurs and CEOs are reading advocates. The more you read, the better you will be at investing, thinking, and developing strategies.

Here is a list of books you should consider reading:

- *The Intelligent Investor* by Benjamin Graham - This book was first released in 1949 and still remains one of the best investment books on the planet. Benjamin Graham was Warren Buffet's college professor, so he definitely knows what he is talking about. It is a dense book, but it is filled with good information. It is a great book to read for overall investing advice.

• *How to Make Money in Stocks: A Winning System In Good Times And Bad* by William J. O'Neil - This is a great skill building book and provides an easy-to follow, seven-step plan to maximize your gains. The information in this book is based on a 100-year study of investors that have turned into stock market winners. It also teaches readers how to avoid common mistakes.

• *One Up On Wall Street* by Peter Lynch - This is not an investment advice book, but rather it is an autobiography. The way the book is written allows the reader to develop their own knowledge about making smart investments. There are many lessons that a reader can take from this book that will help them become better investors. Lynch is one of the most successful investors in the world, so this book is like having him as your personal mentor.

• *Market Wizards* by Jack D. Schwager - The author of this book has gone to the world's top traders and gotten their tips and secrets to be successful in the market. This is an interview style book, which means that the reader gets to hear it straight from the mouths of the professionals. Schwager also boils down the advice given by the professionals into principles that the reader can use in their own lives and trading endeavors.

• *A Random Walk Down Wall Street* by Burton G. Malkiel - Malkiel goes through what he calls the random walk hypothesis, which states that one cannot consistently beat the market. Rather, it is better to build a well-balanced portfolio that can benefit you in the long run. He also goes through both fundamental and technical analysis and some tried and tested investment theories that the reader can implement in their life.

Online Resources and Websites

The internet has provided us with a way to have information right at our fingertips. There is really nothing that you cannot learn from the internet and that is why you should not overlook it. There are many websites and blogs that offer great advice and resources that will help you get better at investing. The great thing about these sites is that they are updated as new information becomes available, so you know that you are getting the most accurate information.

The list I am going to share is not a comprehensive one, as there are probably hundreds of investing advice sites out there. You can always do your own research and find more sites that you enjoy. Just make sure that their advice and guidance is sound. The best sites are the ones that show you where they have gotten their information from and those that cite studies and research. This way you know that the information you are consuming is sound.

- Investopedia: Investing 101 Tutorial - Investopedia is a great website for all things investing. It has great information in its posts and most of it is research-based. This investing tutorial is just one of the many resources you can find on the website. It is filled with great information that will help the novice investor. As you get more experience, you can move on to the more challenging information on the website.

- Yahoo Finance App and Website - This is a great resource for both new and experienced investors. The app allows you to add a list of stocks and then get news streams that are linked to your list. This will help you to stay up-to-date with what is happening in your portfolio.

- Scottrade General Investment Portal - This is one of the investment websites that will allow you to set up a stock simulator to help you get the hang of trading. It also has articles, analysis, and videos that are very helpful for all investors.

- The Motley Fool - This is a long-standing investment website. It has a section for beginners and offers updated news and reports about almost every sector and industry. You will probably be able to find information about the stock you want to invest in on this platform.

- The Money Tree Investing Podcast - This podcast invites guests to talk about different aspects of investing and the stock market. There is also a website that links you up with other important websites and shares book recommendations and other helpful resources.

Online Courses

There are many investment courses available on the internet. Many of them are equivalent to those that you can get at a formal institution, but they are a fraction of the cost. The great thing about these courses is that they give you a lesson plan and access to communities that will help you through the material. There are often lesson videos as well as assignments. This helps solidify the information you are learning. It will also help keep you accountable. If you are someone who struggles to finish books or just leaves things half-done, then these courses are a great option.

For most courses, you will need to pay a fee unless the platform offers a free trial period. They are really not that expensive, and either way, you are more likely to finish something that you have paid for than something that is free as you feel obligated to make your money count. There are many courses being released, so make sure to keep up to date with them. You can also read reviews to make sure that the one you are joining is a good quality one.

- Stock Market From Scratch for Complete Beginners by Udemy - Udemy is a great platform to learn all kinds of things. Experts who just want to share their knowledge create courses for anyone who wants to learn. This particular course is taught by Jatin Taneja, who has years of experience in the field. It is a great course for beginners because he goes through everything from the ground level and then builds up. By the time you are done with this course, you will be well-prepared for the stock market and ready to enter the investing world. He teaches in a style that makes it easy for novices to understand.

- The Investing and Trading Library by TD Ameritrade - This is actually a free option for those who are not too keen on paying for a course. You just need to have an account for the course, and then you can go ahead and start learning. There are tons of resources on the website, and there is even an app that you can download that is very easy to navigate. The courses on the platform are accompanied by webcasts and events that are aimed at helping you achieve your goals.

- Warrior Trading Courses by Warrior Trading - There are actually five different courses that you can take on this website. They cater to everyone from beginner to advanced. It is one of the most comprehensive trading courses out there. You will also have access to chat rooms and to a trading simulator to help you practice what you have learned.

- Stocks, Bonds, and Investing: Oh, My! by The University of Central Florida Online - If you are more interested in learning stocks for the purpose of saving for your retirement or to reach financial goals, then this is the course for you. It does not go in depth about market philosophy and helps you get just the right amount of knowledge to make sure that you know the fundamentals. This is not the course for those who want to become professional traders since it does not go deeply into things like day trading and analytics. This course makes topics interesting and easy to digest for any person at any age. You can learn at your own pace and the course is taught by Matt Crabtree, a Yale alum.

Things You Should Keep in Mind About the Stock Market

The stock market can be an unpredictable place. There is no guarantee of anything, however there are some things that are almost certain. We know this because we can see the trends that happen throughout history, and they always bring us back to the same place. This is reassuring and can help us plan better and have better strategies moving forward.

Staying Calm and Positive Is the Best Strategy

Emotions have no place in the stock market. The farther you can keep them away, the better for you. This will help prevent you from making impulsive decisions, which often results in a negative outcome. If you choose to use logic, you will fare much better. The only way you can do this is by staying calm and positive.

The Numbers Go Up

It is impossible to actually know when a bear market will end, and a bull market will begin. If you are confused by these terms, they are in the list above for you to give yourself a bit of a refresher. You cannot tell when the market will pick back up after a downward trend, and this has been true since the beginning of the stock trade. In most cases, it is not smart to judge future results on past performance, but we have seen this consistently over the years.

In fact, markets often offer their best results after a huge drop. This can be referred to as a market correction. This is why many people go for the long game. The stocks may drop, but eventually, they will pick up again, and you might see the highest prices after this drop.

Automatic Investments

If you really struggle with keeping your emotions in check when it comes to the stock market, an automatic investment might be your ultimate savior. An automatic investment is exactly what it sounds like. You set up an automatic transfer to your investment account for a predetermined amount at a specific time. This allows you to not even look at the stock market and be tempted to sell your shares prematurely. As a result, you don't have to actively take care of your investment portfolio, which is better for some people.

Portfolio Diversification

Even the most experienced trader will get it wrong sometimes. This is mainly because you can never be completely sure of what the market will do. You will probably experience a drop in price for a few of the stocks you invest in. You might even invest in a company that ends up losing you money. This is the nature of stock trading and why we say that there is risk involved.

If you understand the real possibility of losing money on a trade, then you will be able to lessen the risk factor and ensure that you won't lose too much money. The best way to do this is to diversify your portfolio. This just means that you invest in a few different stocks rather than pouring all your money into one stock. If you only choose to invest in one or two stocks, you could end up losing all or most of your money if one of them unexpectedly takes a downward turn. If you have invested in five or six stocks, even if one of them turns out to be a bad investment, you will still have four investments that can cover the cost of the losses from the bad one.

Diversification isn't just about having lots of different stocks. You should still do your research so that you pick ones that you believe will be profitable. You should also try to diversify the sectors in which you invest. This means that you shouldn't just invest in the finance industry or the IT industry. Look for good investments in as many sectors as possible. This includes healthcare, science, manufacturing, and even agriculture. There are plenty of companies in a variety of sectors for you to choose from. If one of the sectors is going through a tough time, you will have investments in other sectors to cover the losses.

Watch Out for These Red Flags

The risks involved with investing in the stock market are not just limited to the stocks themselves. There is also a risk of fraud, which adds another layer of concern to investing. You could become a victim of investment fraud and end up losing your money, and there is no contingency for this. You should do everything in your power to be aware of the signs of fraud and pick up on any red flags. If you are aware, then you will be able to protect yourself and avoid being a victim of investment fraud.

Pushy Stockbrokers

When you are dealing with the stock market, it is better to do so through a stockbroker. Stockbrokers are supposed to help you with your investments and handle your portfolio. However, there are some who are just trying to scam you out of your money. This is why it's important to choose your broker carefully.

There are brokers out there who seem like really nice people who have your best interest at heart but end up manipulating you out of your money. You should always be wary of brokers who are charming and a bit too pushy. If the broker is not listening to your opinions, then you should definitely take that as a red flag.

You should also do some research on the broker and the firm. If you see that they have been under investigation or have had disciplinary hearings, then it is a good idea to not follow through with them. If you have any funny feelings about a specific broker, then it is best to just trust your gut and find someone that you can fully trust. This is your money and your future wealth that you are entrusting to someone, so you need to make sure that they are trustworthy and reliable.

Suspicious Financials

Brokers aren't the only ones who can be guilty of fraud. The company that you are investing in might be up to some fishy business. Businesses might be committing fraud because they are in a competitive market and want to keep their position. It can be difficult to spot fraud if you are the average investor. Some companies are really good at covering up their illicit activities, and even professional accountants can struggle to detect the fraud.

If you invest in a company that is cooking their books and reporting revenue that they haven't actually earned yet, you might end up getting the short end of the stick. While stock prices might look promising now, it can all take a nosedive if such news comes out. It is always best to be cautious and make sure that the companies you invest in have good reputations. You can do this by looking at a company's track record and if they are meeting analysts' profit estimates.

Chapter 4: Proper Analysis Is the Key to Your Success!

Analysis is an important part of stock trading. You should not buy any stock until you have done some sort of analysis. The strategy and the type of stock trading you do will determine how much analysis you will need to do. If you choose to invest, then you will probably only have to do some initial analysis and then leave it at that. If you choose to do something like day trading or swing trading, you will need to do a lot more analysis since you will be constantly trading in the market. Regardless of what you choose, it is good to have some basic knowledge of how to analyze charts and the stock market in general.

What Is a Stock Chart?

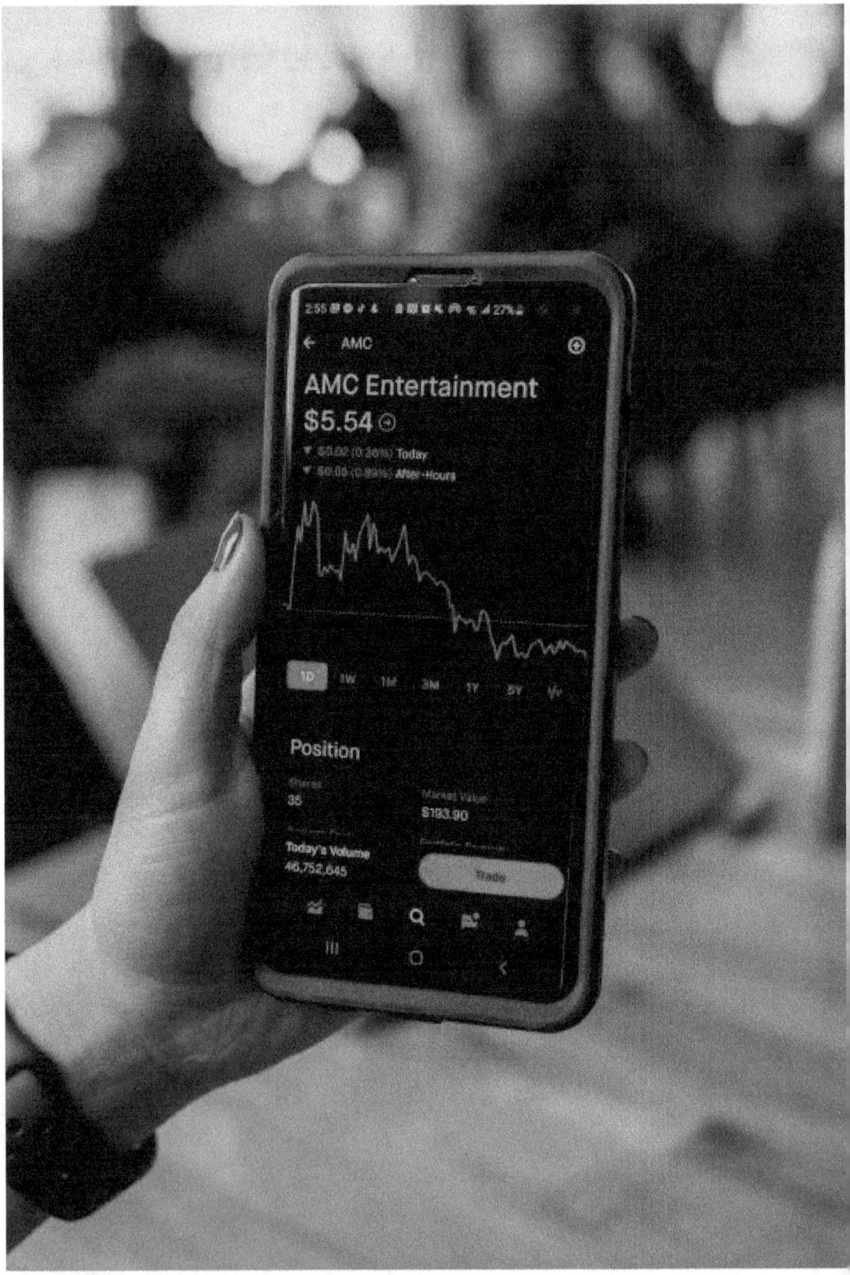

If you want to be able to analyze the stock market, you will need to know how to read a stock chart. A stock chart shows the pricing of the stocks and how they have changed over time. With these charts, you can see when the prices have gone up and when they have fallen.

When you are looking at a chart, you might notice that there are specific times when the price decreases or increases. There can be many reasons for these fluctuations. Sometimes you will be able to pick up on one specific thing that causes the rise or fall in price. If you know what it is, you can predict future increases or decreases. This allows you to make better decisions and can result in the ability to sell your stocks for a great price and profit from that.

There are various charts that you can look at, and each has its own advantages for certain types of trade. The time frame the chart shows is an important thing to consider, and the time frame you should focus on will be determined by the type of trading you are doing. Typically, you will have charts that show daily, weekly, monthly, quarterly, and yearly periods. If you decide to be a short-term trader, then you will be looking at daily charts to see how the prices fluctuate throughout the course of the day. The goal is to buy stocks when they are cheapest and then sell them when they are most expensive, as this will result in the greatest profit for you. If you are a long-term investor, you will be looking at monthly to yearly charts. This will show you big-picture movements so that you can spot the long-term trends taking place in the market.

If you choose day trading, you will have to look at the price change and the last change of the day. The price change has four important points which are the open, high, low, and close. The open is the starting price from the beginning of the day, and the close is the price the stock ends the day on. The high and low are, respectively, the highest and lowest prices the stock reached that day. The last change is whether the stock has seen an overall positive or negative change since the previous day's price. The last change is not only applicable to day trading. You will be able to see the last change based on all time periods.

The other important thing you will see on a chart is the volume. This is the amount of that stock that has been traded in the given time period. If the stock is at a low volume, that means there are few people who are currently trading that stock. This means that the current trend may not continue because there are not enough people trading. If the trading volume is high, it means there are a lot of people buying and selling, and the trend is more likely to continue as is.

Different Types of Stock Charts

When it comes to choosing which of the various types of stock charts you should use, the deciding factors are purpose and preference. These will probably take you back to your school days when you had to plot data on a chart for math class. You will have to read each chart differently as they each present the information in different ways. We will be going through each chart so that you can get a better understanding of them. The four chart types I will talk about are bar charts, candlestick charts, line charts, and point and figure charts.

Let's first start off with the bar chart. On a bar chart you will see multiple price bars. Each one of these bars shows you how the price of that stock has moved over a specific time frame. You can use a bar chart to spot trends and even trend reversals so that you can make the best choices when you are trading or investing. You will see vertical lines that represent the movement of the price. This is usually a jagged line as the price can move up and down quite often. For most bar charts, there is an option to color code it, which makes it much easier to analyze at a glance. Normally, all downward movements would be in red and all upward movements would be in green. Many people choose to use a bar chart because it is quite simple to read, and they are familiar with the format, since it is a common way to make charts in other areas that use them.

Candlestick charts are interesting because they show how the emotions of traders can influence the price movement. This is done by visually representing the size of the movements using colors. With this kind of chart, you will be using the candlesticks to make directions based on previous trends that you have seen on the chart. The candlestick chart will show the exact same information as the bar chart, so which one you should use depends on what you prefer to look at. The candlesticks are much thicker, so they are more visual. If you need to have a good visual representation of something, then a candlestick chart might be your go-to.

Another choice to consider is the line chart. This is a common type of chart that you would have seen in many other situations throughout your life. It is a popular choice because it clearly shows you the movement of the information you are tracking. Instead of having multiple lines showing each movement individually, a line graph just uses one line to show continuous movement. It is a great choice for getting an overall look at how the stock is moving in the market, but its simplistic nature does pose a challenge when trying to pick out individual trends. Day traders don't often use this type of chart because it is too simple and does not give enough detailed information. Line charts typically only show closing prices, so you will be able to see the overall increase or decrease in price. This makes line charts useful for long-term investors.

The final chart you should know about is the point and figure chart. This type of chart plots the price movements without considering the period of time that has passed. It does this by using stacked Xs and Os in columns to show data. Each X or O represents a set amount of price movement. Xs are typically in green, representing an increase in price and Os in red, representing a decrease in price. These Xs and Os are stacked on top of each other to show the movements of the price. So there would be a stack of Xs showing an upward movement and a stack of Os showing a downwards movement. This chart filters out tiny price movements, which means that they are less likely to show a false trend.

Components of a Stock Chart

There are seven main components of any stock chart. These components build the chart and help the reader to understand what the chart is trying to convey. These seven components are the chart type, timescale (x-axis), price scale (y-axis), on-chart indicators, off-chart indicators, time frames, and drawing tools. I have already gone through the chart types, so instead of rehashing those, I will discuss each of the other components in detail so that you can understand what you are looking at when you have a chart in front of you.

The time scale is the x-axis of the chart. If you remember from school, the x-axis is the horizontal line at the bottom of the chart. As you move farther to the right, the time frame gets larger. This timescale will show the time that you have chosen to look at, so the extent of the scale depends on whether you are short-term or long-term trading. The price scale is the y-axis, which is the vertical line on the right side of the chart. As you go up this line, you will see that the price increases. Everything within the chart will fall in between these two lines and the data that can be found on them.

The on-chart indicators are the indicators that you will plot on your chart. The aim of this is to have some visual parameters for the price movement on the chart. You would be able to draw on the chart and see things like whether the stock finds support at a 100-day average. When placing indicators on a chart, it is important to note that less really is more, and you should not overdo it, otherwise you risk confusing yourself.

Off-chart indicators are used to show you oversold or overbought levels of a specific stock. Volume, which we spoke about in the previous section, is a good off-chart indicator. Volume allows you to see the supply and demand of the stock, and while it is not on the main chart, it is still a valuable piece of information. Off-chart indicators often give additional information to what is shown on the chart and can usually be found in a section just below the chart itself.

The final two components are time frames and drawing tools. You choose the time frames. This is just the amount of time you want to see data for and can be anywhere from an hour all the way to several years. The length depends on the type of trading or investing you are doing in the stock market. Drawing tools allow you to formulate your own ideas on the chart. You can draw boundaries to encapsulate certain trading activity that you deem important to you. There are quite a few drawing tools to use, and you can use them as you wish. The most popular tool is lines. You can play around with the tools until you find what works for you.

How to Read a Stock Chart

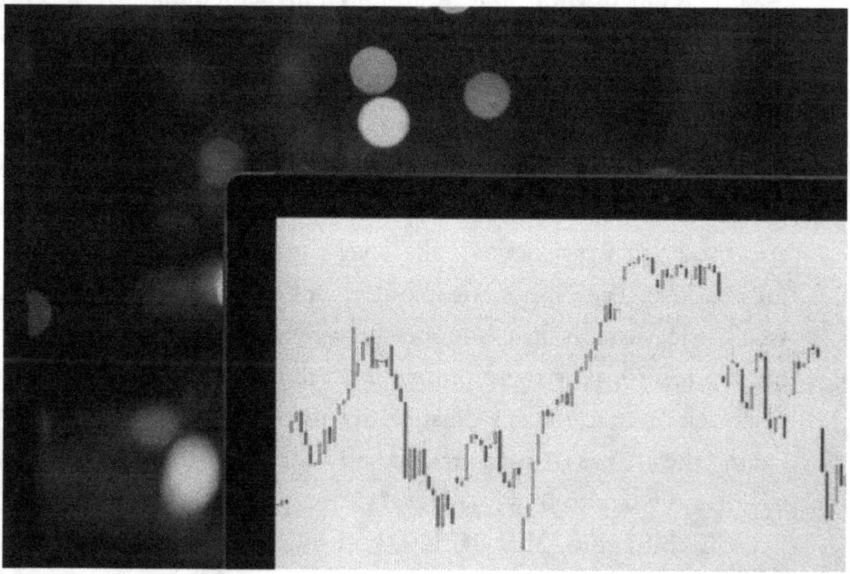

When you are reading a stock chart, you are probably investing in individual stocks. This is where this skill comes in handy. Index and mutual funds don't really require much analysis, so if you are choosing to invest in one of these, you don't have to do much analysis and won't have to read charts. However, if you are planning to move into investing in individual stocks at some point, then you should still learn to analyze charts.

A stock chart is simply a chart with all the historical information of the movements of your chosen stock in the time frame that you have stipulated. Knowing how to read this chart will allow you to make better decisions in the future by analyzing what was going on in the stock's past. There are four important things that you need to know about when it comes to reading a stock chart.The first one is identifying the trend line, which is the main line that you will see when you have a stock chart, and this is especially so on line charts. If you Google any company's stock price, the first thing that will pop up is a chart with one line that shows the up and down movements of the stock price. This line is the trend line. If you notice any huge gains or drops at a specific point in time, you should do a little digging to find out what happened at that point. This will help you to figure out if this will happen again and when it will probably happen.

The next thing you will have to look at is the lines of support and resistance. These are the levels at which the stock stays for a given period. A line of support is the price the stock is not likely to go below and the line of resistance is the level the stock is likely not going to move above. These lines create buffers for you to work within and the stock price usually just bounces between these two lines. The stock price can push past these buffers if there is a huge change that causes the stock price to make a drastic movement on either side. The goal of having these lines of support and resistance is so that you know when to sell and when to buy.

The third thing that is important to know is when dividends and stock splits happen. You will be able to see this information at the bottom of a chart. It will show you in which time period either of these two things took place. You can then look at the stock price and the trends that followed to see how the market reacted to this change. We have already spoken about dividends, so I will not be going into it here. A stock split is a strategic move that is issued by the directors of the company that allows more shares to be available. If you already own shares, you will have more shares when the stock has been split. For example, if you own 100 shares of a company, and it does a split of 5:1, you will then have 500 shares of that company. While the value of the company does not change (nor does the total value of the stock you hold), the individual stock price does. The reason this split is done is that the directors feel that the share price is not in line with their competitors' or to allow smaller investors the opportunity to invest in the company. In most cases, the share prices will increase after a stock split because there are more people interested in investing in that company. However, you have to keep in mind that the price might decline initially if you already own shares in that company. Thus, it would not be a good time to sell, and it is usually better to just wait until the price picks back up.

The final thing that you will need to take into account when you are reading a stock chart is the historic trading volumes. You will be able to see trading volumes at the bottom of your screen, right below the chart. It is good to keep trading volumes in mind, but they should not be the only thing you look at when you are investing in a stock. High trading volume does not necessarily mean that the stock price will increase. This is why you should always look at how the trading volume affected the stock price in the past. This will give you a better idea of how it will react in the future, and you will be able to make more accurate decisions.

Market Timing

While the buy-and-hold strategy has been a popular one for a long time now, many people are looking into a more strategic approach to investing. This is whether you are interested in long-term investments or short-term ones. It is always good to know an alternative strategy and try it out as it might end up resulting in greater profits. This is not to say that the buy-and-hold strategy is a bad one; in the long term, it is actually a great strategy, but if you understand how to time the market, you might just get better returns.

If you are trying to time the market, you should take a few steps so that you can do it properly. The first thing that you need to do is study long-term cycles in the market. Look at how the stock market as a whole performed in various years in the past. See if you can pinpoint any reasons for the rise or fall in stock prices. Long-term market forces are things like interest rate fluctuations, inflation, and regular currency trends. These big things can definitely have an impact on the stock market, and if you can see this coming, then you can make your trading or investing decisions with this in mind. You should also keep the time of the year in mind because different strategies may work better at certain times of the year. Certain stocks do better at a specific time of the year as well. Something that has been noticed in regard to tech stocks is that they do better in the first half of the year and taper off mid-summer, and there are plenty of other stocks and sectors that act like this at specific points in the year. It is good to know when these are so that you can choose to buy and sell at the right times.

You should always keep your eye on the stock's support and resistance levels. The best time to buy a stock is when it is closest to the support line. This is when the stock is at the lowest price you can expect. Usually, the stock price will go up from here and this is good news whether you are planning for short-term results or a long-term investment. Along with this, you should be looking out for correlated markets. The modern market environment is made up of rotational strategies in correlated sectors. This means that something that happens in a sector that might seem unrelated might end up affecting the sector your stock is in. You should always be studying both your sector and one that is correlated to yours to make sure that you are not caught off guard by any changes.

You may want to hold for a long time, and this can be a good strategy, but you should always have an exit strategy in place. You should identify a capitulation price for your position so that if things do start taking a nosedive, you will be able to get out rather than just hoping things will get better. For your long-term investments, you should consider having a multi-year position which reaches a historic high. A strong resistance level that has been going on for a while might be the mark of a market turn that could last for many years into the future. This is not something that you want to be caught up in, so it might make more sense to sell and invest that money in more solid long-term opportunities. Taking the time to readjust your strategy is important when you are placing your money in the stock market.

Price Prediction

When you are trying to predict prices, the best way to go about it is through technical analysis. If you know how to read charts and know about technical analysis, you should have a good idea of how to predict prices and your predictions will be a lot more accurate. It is important to note that no matter how much you prepare or how good your prediction is, there is still a chance of it not turning out the way you thought it would. This is just the nature of stock trading, so you have to take your knocks along with the wins.

Prices can actually do much more than just going up and down. They could chop sideways or whipsaw. These might be foreign terms to you, but I will be explaining them shortly. It is important to know what these are so that you can make more accurate predictions and get the result that you want.

Chopping Sideways

A sideways trend is a result of the up and down movement of the stock that stays between the levels of support and resistance. Even though it is still moving up and down, it is moving in a predictable manner and that shows that the levels of supply and demand are balanced. After this period there is often a period of more pronounced increase or decrease, which can be capitalized on, depending on the direction of the movement.

It is not uncommon to see a prolonged period of this sideways movement. This can go on for days and even months, depending on the market. If you have shares in this stock and want to sell, you should set a stop loss at the resistance level so that you can get the most out of selling that stock. Once this sideways trend is done, there will be a bigger increase or decrease in the stock price. This will lead to another sideways movement. If you look at a chart, you will see that the stock had been chopping sideways many times during an extended time frame.

Whipsawing

Whipsawing is something that happens quite often, but it can be an unexpected event. It is when there is a trend in a certain direction and then suddenly it moves in the opposite direction. This means there are only two ways for a stock to whipsaw. The first is for a stock to be constantly moving in an upward direction and then suddenly dropping below its original price. The second way a stock whipsaws is by being on a downward trend and then suddenly shooting upward above the original price. If you own shares, you probably hope for the second example to become a reality.

The problem with a whipsaw event is that it is unpredictable. This means that there is no standard way of dealing with it. You could end up at a loss or be surprised that the stock price suddenly shot up. You will have to decide what to do when you are in the situation, but if the price drops very low, then it would probably be best to ride out the low point. In most cases, the share prices do climb back up after an unexpected downturn, so if you have the patience for it, you should try to wait it out. An upward whipsaw is also tricky to detect. You don't know if the price will drop back down quickly or if it will stay quite high and then keep moving up. You would have to do some research and analysis of your own to find out whether it would be better to sell at the top of a whipsaw or to wait it out and see if you can make an even bigger profit.

Making Trading Predictions Based on Trends

When owning a share or wanting to buy one, there are two prices that are important to know, these are the current price and the future selling price. In order to make a profit, you will need the future selling price to be higher than the price you bought it for. On top of that, you don't want it to just be a little higher; you want it to be high enough to cover any fees you have incurred throughout the trading process and for it to be worth your while. There is no way to know the exact future selling price, but you can do a very good job of predicting it so that you know you can have peace of mind that you are making a good investment.

There really is no right answer to predicting the market, even after years of research. This means that every person has to find a strategy and go with it for as long as it is working for them. There are four common factors that people use to predict the market. I will go through these factors, and then you can decide which one is best for you to implement.

The first of the four is momentum. The logic behind this is actually rooted in behavioral psychology. People are more likely to invest in a stock that is moving upwards than one that is staying low or has hit a downward trend. The reason for this is that there are so many stocks in the market that, if you have to pick one, you will more likely pick the one that is already showing positive movement. This means that if a stock is moving up then there is a high chance that it will continue to do that for some time due to the demand for it increasing. A study that was done on this showed that the effect only lasted for about 3 to 12 months, so it is not a good indicator of long-term upward movements. Stocks that have done well in the time frame of three to five years will often underperform in the next three to five years, and then the cycle repeats itself (Yates, 2021).

The next factor is mean reversion, which is the belief that the market will eventually even itself out over time. People who have been investing in the stock market for a long time believe this because they would have seen it happen multiple times. This is why experienced investors shy away from investing when the stock prices are high and use low stock prices as an opportunity to start buying. A high price means that the stock price will eventually come back down to the mean level, which means it would be a bad time to invest. A low stock price indicates a good time to invest because the price will eventually move back up to the mean level. This is not an exact science, but it has worked for many people. There have been no conclusive studies done to show whether this works the majority of the time. That is why most people who opt to use this as an indicator to time the market are those who have experienced this type of thing while they were trading and have drawn their conclusions from there.

Martingales is another factor that people use to try to predict the market. A martingale is just a mathematical principle that states the best predictor of what the next number in a series will be is the current number. If you use this principle, you will not be taking into account the past or any historic return that you have seen in the market for your specific stock. Despite there being some short-term backward movements, the overall trend will be consistently higher. The thought pattern behind this is that if the stock market is completely random, then it does not matter what happened in the past. The best thing to do, then, is focus on how to manage the inherent risk of investing in the stock market, and this will give you the best returns in the long run.

The final thing that can help with predicting the market is the search for value. When you are a value investor, you aim to purchase a stock at a cheap price with the expectation of a reward later on down the line. The hope here is that the market is performing inefficiently and that it will adjust itself over time so that the stock price better reflects the value of the company the shares belong to. This readjustment is constantly happening in the stock market, so this belief is well-founded. The trick is to pick a stock that is actually undervalued. This requires some research on your part. If you are able to find an undervalued stock, all that is left to do is wait for the market to correct itself, and then you will be rewarded for it.

Chapter 5: Practice Before You Preach

Practicing may not be the most fun part of the whole trading experience, but it is definitely necessary. Many people think that they can just skip practicing when they have started trading for real, but you should always be practicing. It will help you build up your skill level and also help you make fewer mistakes when you are risking your money.

Why You Should Practice Trading

Practicing is important for all types of trading, but it is definitely more so when it comes to day trading. This is a skill that has to be continuously worked on, like most skills. A professional athlete does not stop practicing when they have made it into the Olympics. Instead, they practice harder and hone their skills so that they keep getting better. This should be the mindset of a trader as well.

If you are a day trader or thinking about becoming one, something that you should keep in mind is that it is super fast-paced. You have to think quickly and then be quick to react. This is the only way that you will be able to make a good amount of money doing this. The only way that you will get faster and teach yourself to think quicker is to practice, which is why it should be a priority for you.

Practicing can also help you get attuned to the market. This is essential for all types of trading. The more you put yourself in the market, the better your chances of predicting future outcomes. The best way to make sure that you are making the right choices is to make sure that you are familiar with the market and how it works. You can read about the stock market all you like, but until you really dive in, certain things will never click, and you will not have the experience needed to make smart choices.

I have already mentioned the role of emotions when it comes to trading. It is easy to get caught up in emotions, and then you end up making bad decisions based on that. Even if you are not an emotional person, or you think that you will be able to keep your emotions in check, I hate to break it to you, but keeping your emotions out of your trades isn't a simple matter. This takes practice because you need to be aware of the emotions you feel when you win or lose. This is only something you can get better at through practice and continuously analyzing yourself and your reactions. It is so much better to figure this out through practicing with a simulation rather than in the real market where your emotions will be heightened because you have real money on the line.

Another benefit to practicing is that you will be able to find your trading style. You can have all the information in the world, but the fact is that everyone has their own trading style. The people who are successful are those who follow their own style rather than copying from others. The only way you will be able to find your style is to keep trading. If you do this in tandem with actually trading in the market, you will be able to get better and then make changes to your market stocks based on what you have discovered while practicing.

You will get better the more you practice. This is true for every area of life, and trading in the stock market is no different. You will thank yourself for putting in that extra time to practice and allow yourself to learn. Furthermore, you will be able to formulate a better plan with the knowledge you have gained and then reap the rewards in the stock market.

How to Practice Trading

Now that you know the importance of practice, you need to know how to do it. The way you do this is by paper trading, which may sound strange, but it is just using a trading simulator. The name paper trading goes back all the way to when people used to practice trading on paper before they entered live markets. We are a little more sophisticated now, and you can practice using online simulators. This is much easier than actually using paper, and you will be able to get a full trading experience without the risk of losing any money.

When you sign up for one of these trading simulators, you will be given a certain amount of fake money. This is what you will use to play around with. This money has no real-world value, so you will not gain any profits or suffer any losses from whatever happens in the simulation. It is designed to be a no-risk way of building up your confidence and gaining the skills you need to enter the real stock market.

Many trading simulators ask you to pay some sort of fee to gain access. The reason for this fee is that you will have access to a lot of other resources that will help you grow in your skill set. This will allow you to get a better education in trading and the stock market. This is worth the fee you will have to pay as you can possibly make more than that back when you actually start trading. If you are not keen on paying a fee, then there are also some great free options, which I will tell you about soon.

There are also many stockbrokers who will offer their clients paper trading accounts. If you are signing up with a broker, ask them if they can provide this for you. This is also a great way to tell if the brokerage is legitimate and actually wants you to succeed. This may not be a foolproof way to tell, but it is certainly something to look out for. Your broker will then be able to guide you through the system and answer any questions you have. When you are comfortable with the simulation, you can move onto the real thing.

If you are looking for a good and reliable paper trading app or website, take a look at this list:

- TD Ameritrade thinkorswim's paperMoney
- Webull
- TradeStation
- MarketWatch's Virtual Stock Exchange
- Investopedia's Stock Simulator
- Wealthbase
- Wall Street Survivor
- HowTheMarketWorks

The first six are all apps that can be downloaded on your phone or computer. I suggest using your chosen program on your computer as that is where you will be doing your trading. The best part about those six apps is that they are free, so you won't have to be out of pocket when you are doing your practice runs. The last two on the list are trading simulators that have a lot of added features that will help you along your trading journey. They give you access to quizzes and journals, among other resources. These are really helpful, and you will be able to jumpstart your trading career with all of this at your fingertips.

Pros and Cons of Paper Trading

Paper trading is definitely something that everyone who wants to get into the market should do. It helps you get familiar with the system, and you will be able to hone your skills. However, it wouldn't be fair to just talk about how good paper trading is without balancing it out with some of the downsides. There is nothing inherently bad about paper trading, but there are some limitations, and you should be aware of these so that you know where paper trading will fit into your strategy.

Let's first talk about the pros, as there are quite a few. I have already touched on some of them throughout this chapter, so I won't repeat those. The number one pro is that it allows you to practice in a risk-free environment. This is the major draw to paper trading and why traders should take part in it. Not only that, but it also removes the stress from the situation. Since you are not using your own money, you are less likely to stress out over your next move. This allows you to think more clearly, and as a beginner you can focus on more of the strategy.

A huge benefit of paper trading is that it allows the trader to see statistics on their strategies. This is good for the advanced trader and the beginner alike. If you are thinking about trying out a new strategy, you can do it on a paper trading platform, and then after a few weeks, you will gain valuable statistics and feedback from your new strategy. From here, you can decide whether it will work or you need to change something about it. The more you paper trade, the more confidence you will build before you go out into the stock market. This confidence is great for beginners and for more experienced traders who are looking to make a change to their market approach.

The cons or the limitations of paper trading are definitely something to keep in mind. These do not discredit the platform, but you should not overuse it for these reasons. The first con is that it is not directly correlated to the market. Paper trading does not address the broad market effects on each individual stock. This does not give a completely accurate view on what is happening in the actual stock market. You will also have to be aware that paper trading does not come with any hidden costs, but trading in the stock market does. Many people are surprised when they move over to trading in the stock market because of the fees they have incurred that they were never trained for with paper trading.

While we mentioned that the emotions are taken out of the equation when you are paper trading as a pro, it can also be a negative thing. Emotions really do play a huge role in trading in the stock market. If you do not get exposure to that part of it, you will not know how to handle it. Practicing is important, but you should be aware that the real thing will be different, so you will not be able to go all in when you do start trading for real. When you are paper trading, things are a little more structured, and it is easier to pick out ideal entry and exit points. This is not the same with real-world trading. There are many more factors that you will have to consider and that does add challenges to the process.

Paper trading is a valuable asset to your trading journey, but is not exactly what you will be facing in real-world trading situations. There is a lot of volatility and hidden costs to real-world trading that you won't be exposed to when you are paper trading. It is for this reason that you should not think that whatever you are able to accomplish when you are paper trading you will be able to replicate identically in a real-world situation. It is always good to practice and be as prepared as possible but also expect the real thing to have different challenges.

How to Manage Your Money

If you follow all the tips in this book and start trading, then you will be making some extra money. This will look different for everyone, but one thing that you must pay attention to is how you manage your money. The greatest and most successful people in the world don't gain that status by just simply investing. They also know how to manage their money well. All the gain you have made through trading or investing can eventually amount to nothing if it is not managed well. You want to have long-term wealth, not just short-term money that is eventually lost.

If you want to manage your money well, there are a few things that must be done. You will need to manage all of your money well and not just the money that you gain in the stock market. Money management is about having the right habits in place so that you can keep track of your money and spend it in the smartest way possible. While it may sound like fun to blow all your newly earned money on cars and vacations to tropical destinations, this will not allow you to make the best use of your money. The fun stuff will come, but first, you must have the right structures in place that will give you the freedom to buy the extras while still having security for the future.

Make Sure You Have a Budget

Budgeting is the cornerstone of money management. Many people do not do this because they don't want to go through what might seem like a lengthy process of writing down all their expenses and matching it up to their income. Budgets help us to stay on track, and while it may not be fun, it is necessary. Those who do not have proper budgets in place do not spend their money well and are more likely to end up blowing it on things that are not important.

When you create your budget, you should have a list of priorities. These are the things that absolutely have to be paid off. Rent, food, savings, car payments, and debt payments are examples of things that would fall in the nonnegotiable category. The next list would be things that are important but are not life or death. This could be the amount of extra money you want to invest in the stock market, fun money, or perhaps you need a pair of shoes for an event or for work. These types of things can change every month. After you have paid off all the important things, you can divide the remaining money into the other categories. If you do not have enough money for the less important things, you will have to leave them until the next month. You should also make sure that there is a certain amount set aside for unbudgeted expenses. Things pop up, but you need to have something set aside for these things so that you don't overspend. Once you have set your budget, you need to make sure that you stick to it.

Track Your Spending

Once you have made your budget, the only way you can be sure to stick to it is to track your spending. This means that you will have to either write down or take note of every single thing you buy. Every time you spend money, you need to record it. Then you need to place the items in your budget categories to make sure that you are not overspending in each area. Doing this is the only way you can be sure that you are sticking to the budget.

Hold off on the Big Purchases

When it comes to big purchases, it is always better to save up for a few months and then buy. This allows us to not break the bank for these items and helps us to learn how to delay gratification. We often want things now, but this can be a disadvantage. There will be many things in life that will need us to pause and delay gratification for a while. The better you are at this, the better you will be able to manage your money and other areas of your life.

Saving up will also stop you from putting things on credit. While credit might seem like a good idea in the short term, it actually costs you more in the end. Interest can really add up, and that is extra money that you could be investing or saving. Most big purchases do not need to be bought right now. If you;ve lived without it until now, there is a good chance that you could do the same for a few more months.

Remember to Save

Saving is an important habit that can actually help you build wealth for the future. We should all have savings accounts that we contribute to every month and should be at the top of the list of priorities. The big mistake people make is that they spend their money first then say that they will save whatever is left. There will always be things to buy, so you won't actually end up with any savings. This is why saving must be done first. If you find it hard to save, you can set up an automatic transfer into your savings account so that you don't even have to think about it.

There are two important types of savings accounts you should have. The first is an emergency fund, and the other is for long-term savings. An emergency fund is an easily accessible account you can pull money from just in case you need it. You never know what might happen, and it is good to have some money saved up to handle life's unexpected situations. Your long-term savings can be placed in a fixed savings account that cannot be accessed until a certain time period has lapsed. You will gain more interest from these types of accounts, and these are for long-term savings like retirement or for your children's college expenses.

Get Out of Debt

If you are in debt, then this is the most important step of managing your money. You have to get out of debt to truly enjoy financial freedom. Borrowed money comes with some hefty interest rates and fees, and the longer you have the debt, the more you will pay. All of this added interest is money that you could be investing or saving. The quicker you get out of debt, the better, so focus all your attention on getting it done. Once you are out of debt, do your best to not buy unnecessarily on credit and plan for the big expenses so that you do not have to borrow money.

If you want to get out of debt, you will need a plan. It is not enough to simply put any extra money you have into paying off your debt. Write down all the debt you have and the interest rates that each one carries. From here you should choose one account to focus your attention on, while still paying the minimum amounts on all the rest. This way you can start paying off your debt more quickly while staying current on the rest.

There are two ways you can pay off your debt efficiently. The first is to start with the smallest account. Once that is paid off, you can take the money you were paying for it and put it into the next smallest account. You can keep doing this, and it will create a snowball effect until all your debt is paid off.

The second option is to pay off the account with the highest interest rate first. Once that is paid off you can move on to the second highest and so forth. This does take longer to gain momentum, but in the long run you will end up paying back less money since you are removing the accounts with the highest interest rates. Both of these methods work well, so you should choose the one that works for you. If you need to see things happening in order to be motivated, then the first one will be a better fit since you will be able to cross off a few accounts early on in the debt payment process.

Set Financial Goals

Goals help us to see what is important to us and then make a plan to reach them. If we do not have goals and priorities in place, we can end up spending our money on things that are not important. When you are setting your financial goals, you need to decide what is most important to you. Everyone should be saving up for retirement, so that should definitely be a priority. Other things that could be a priority for you could be traveling, buying a house or car, paying off a student loan, or funding the start of a business.

Write down your top three to five goals and then make a plan to reach them. This will allow you to say 'no' to certain things so that you have enough money for the most important things. For example, if you do not like cleaning and are tempted to hire a cleaning service for your house but know that you are saving towards a house, you will be able to forgo cleaning service and put the money towards the house fund.

Once you have set your goals, make sure that you are keeping track of how close you are getting. Celebrating the progress is a great way to keep you motivated to keep going. Setting financial goals is one of the most important things you can do for your financial health. Your goals might change over time, so you should revisit your goals at least every year so that you can keep them up to date.

Chapter 6: Ready for the Big Bucks? Time to Open an Account

Now that you know the basics of investing, the only thing left to do is open an account and get going. That sentence might sound like it is a very easy thing to do, but there are some things that you need to consider when you open your account. I am going to take you through these things so that you are able to open your account with ease and make the right choices along the way.

Choosing Your Advisor

There are three distinct types of advisors that you could go with when you enter the stock market. These are robo-advisors, online brokers, or a traditional financial manager. They will help you with all of your decisions. Each of these has its own set of pros and cons that you should consider before you decide which one is for you.

Robo-Advisor

Robo-advisors have changed the way we do things because before, the only opinion was to have an in-person human advisor. Traditional financial planners are usually much more expensive than robo-advisors, so if you are looking to save some money or just don't have a lot of money to fund your stock market career, then this is a great option.

A robo-advisor is not an actuarial robot that comes out to help you whenever you call it. We aren't that advanced yet. It is actually just a computer algorithm that is used to build and manage your investment and trading portfolio. There is very little interaction that needs to be done from your side. All you have to do is set the parameters for it to work in, and you will be good to go. If you are looking for some investment management but do not need any financial advice or planning, then this will be a great option for you. It is also great for those you are trying to work on a budget.

A robo-advisor is great for passive investing, but it is not designed to beat the market. So if you are interested in short-term trading, then this is not the option for you. Long-term investments and the buy-and-hold strategy is where the robo-investors shine. In the long term, your investments will grow, and you won't pay a lot in fees, which means your profit margin should be quite high.

Online Broker

If you are very comfortable managing your own trades, then an online brokerage might be the best choice for you. With an online broker, you will be buying stocks online instead of on the phone with an actual broker or in person at their office. You call all the shots, and you can choose whether you run passively or actively.

This also means that it is up to you to rebalance the portfolio and make the right choices. There isn't anyone you can get advice from, and you won't be relying on a computer algorithm, like with a robo-advisor. If you want more support, then you need to get a human broker you can communicate with over the phone. This broker can give you advice on your portfolio and, with your permission, purchase and sell stocks. An actual broker will be more costly than an online broker.

Financial Manager

A financial manager is the most comprehensive of all of these advisors. They are hired to help their clients with all aspects of their finances or specific ones that the client outlines. This means that the financial advisor will have access to all of your financial records and will be able to help you make the best decisions based on where you are financially. The other types of advisors focus solely on the stock market side of things, which means that they would help you decide on what stocks to pick based only on the stock market and your goals. A financial manager has a bigger-picture view and can give you advice based on all the factors of your financial situation. If you do not have any money to play with at the moment, the advisor might tell you to hold off on investing in the stock market, and if you have a surplus, they might tell you how much of it to place in the market. Of course, all these benefits make hiring a financial manager more expensive than the other options.

You will be able to discuss your goals and the time frame in which you want to reach them with your financial advisor. They would then develop a plan to help you meet those goals. This plan would include budgeting, monitoring your accounts and spending habits, finding the best investment opportunities for you, creating contingency plans for unexpected circumstances, and reevaluating the financial plan every so often to make sure that it is still meeting your needs in the best way possible. They will also be able to purchase stocks and bonds on your behalf, so all aspects of your finances will be taken care of. You will be able to call them for advice whenever you need them and build a relationship with your financial manager over time.

Stock Brokerage Firms

If you have decided to go with a stock brokerage firm, then you will want to pick a good one. The problem is that there are so many out there, it can be difficult to make a choice. You will definitely have to do your research to make sure that the one you choose is the right fit for you, but to make that process easier, here is a list of the best online brokerage firms provided by Voigt (2021b):

- TD Ameritrade
- SoFi Active Investing
- Interactive Brokers IBKR Lite
- J. P. Morgan Self-Directed Investing
- Zacks Trade
- E*TRADE
- Ally Invest
- Merrill Edge
- Vanguard
- Fidelity
- Charles Schwab

To give you a better understanding of these brokerages, let's go through a few pros and cons of a few of the most popular ones. SoFi is a great option for beginners who do not have a lot of money to pour into investing. They offer the basic services that will allow the investor to create a good portfolio with either a passive or active strategy. More advanced features like stop loss are not offered here, which is a definite downside.

YouInvest is a service by JP Morgan, which is a very well known investment company. It offers commission-free trading of US stocks and bonds and has a great digital platform. The downsides are that it does not have a lot of available tools and its product portfolio is quite limited.

Ally Invest is also commission free and there is no minimum amount needed to open an account. This makes it ideal for a beginner who is looking to get started with a small amount. The cons are that mutual funds have a transaction fee, that you can't trade futures on the platform.

TD Ameritrade actually offers a wide variety of features and stock options, and the customer support is great. The only downside is that it does not offer fractional shares, which is not too much of a concern, especially if you are a beginner.

The final brokerage I will touch on is E*TRADE. This is a brokerage that offers low trading fees and has some great research tools. The downsides here are that it does not offer forex and the live chat function is pretty slow.

Picking a Broker You Can Trust

It is very important that you pick a stockbroker that you can trust and that is actually legitimate. While all the ones I have mentioned are great choices, you should still do your own research, and if you want to pick a broker that is not on the list, then you will need to know how.

The first thing you will need to do to make sure your broker is trustworthy is do a little research on them. Go online and check their reviews. You should always do this on independent review sites as these will be the most trustworthy. If the majority of the reviews are positive, then you know they are probably a good choice. You can then go to the SEC, where all licensed brokers must be registered. You can browse its database and find all the records on the brokerage, including any disciplinary action that has been taken out against it.

While you are doing your research, don't be afraid to ask other people for their input. You should always ask people you know and trust. The best recommendations come from people who use the broker, so you know that they are reliable and trustworthy. Once all of your research is done, it is time to talk to your potential broker directly. Ask them as many questions as you see fit, and you will get a good sense of whether they are competent or not. There is a lot you can tell from speaking to someone directly. Once you are happy, you can go ahead with your chosen broker.

Beginner Mistakes to Avoid

When you are just starting out, there will be many possible mistakes you can make. I am going to go through the top three that you should be aware of and avoid in order to give yourself the best start in the market.

Buying Stock Based on Recommendations

When we first start out, it can be easy to turn to our friends and family for investing advice. This is not necessarily a bad thing, but when you base all your buying decisions on what other people are doing, there will be a problem. Everyone has different risk tolerances and goals, so buying just because someone else has invested in that stock may be a bad idea for you. As I have mentioned earlier, trading in the stock market does not have a one size fits all approach to it. Take in all the advice you can, but then sit down, do your own research, measure the advice against your goals, and then make your choice.

Getting Emotionally Invested in the Company

The emotional side of the stock market is not just about the price of the stocks but also about the companies themselves. It can be easy to get so invested in a company's mission, brand, and goals, that you are blind to all the red flags. When you invest in the stock market, you shouldn't buy a stock because you have an emotional tie to the company. This would be a very bad move. You need to invest in companies that will give you the best returns, even if you do not buy into their brands. A Samsung user can still invest in Apple because they see that Apple will be a good investment for future growth even if they do not like Apple's products. Make sure that you are staying up to date with what is going on with the companies you have invested in and don't be afraid to sell if you see red flags popping up.

Chasing High Returns

Investing in a company just because it is giving you high returns at that point is a bad investment strategy. Stock movements are cyclical, so what is giving high returns now will probably hit a downturn, so if you only chase the highs, you will more than likely get burned. You need to be willing to ride the ups and downs of the stock market and not just jump in when things are good. Remember that if you invest at a low point and the stock climbs, you will get a better profit than going for something that already has high returns and risks hitting a downward trend.

Trading and Taxes

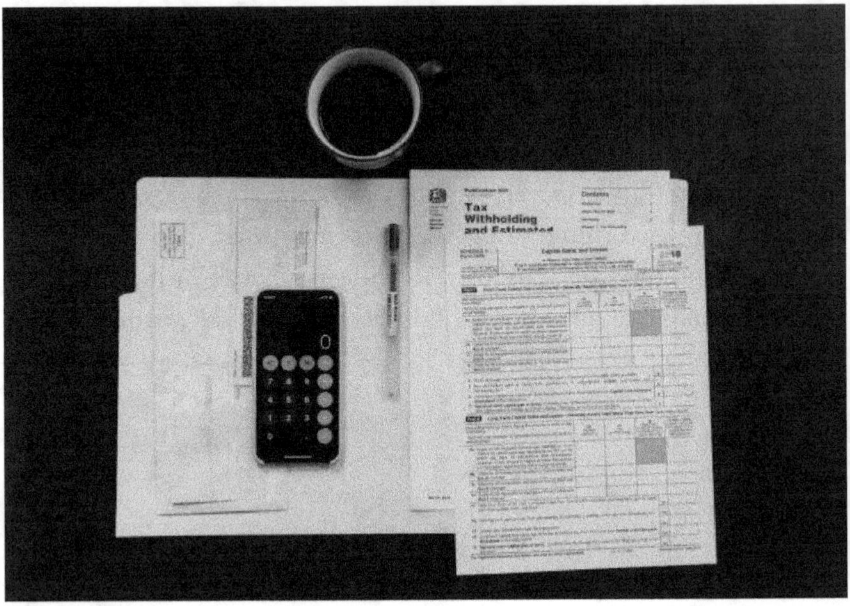

Taxes are a big part of trading, so make sure that you do your research on what that implies in your country or state. Every time you trade a stock, you might need to pay capital gains tax. This is something to keep in mind and is the reason that you shouldn't be making moves that only promise small returns. One of the ways you can lessen the amount of tax you pay is to purchase your stocks through a tax-deferred account. This kind of account makes it so you will not be taxed on your stock trades until you withdraw the money. If you use the account as a retirement fund, your tax rate will be much lower when you retire than it is now.

You can also reduce the amount of capital gains tax you pay by investing any dividends you receive back into the fund. This way, you don't have to keep paying taxes on the dividends; however, it does mean that you will not be able to use the money in the present. If you hold your stocks for a long time and let them grow, you will end up paying less tax in the long run. Short-term capital gains are taxed as ordinary income, which comes with a much higher tax rate. Long-term capital gains are taxed at a much lower rate, and you will end up saving a lot of money.

There are lots of ways for you to avoid paying extremely high taxes. Since you will ultimately be taxed on the income you make from your stocks, you should do your best to make sure that you pay the lowest possible amount. This allows you to have a higher profit margin. If you do not know how to go about declaring your taxes, you can hire a tax consultant to help you. They will also be able to find ways to lessen the tax burden and help you through the whole process.

Opening Your Account

Now it is time to open your brokerage account. Many people think this is a difficult task, but it does not have to be if you know what to do from the beginning. Before you do anything else, you have to determine the type of account that you need. If you have a short-term goal in mind, you can go for a standard brokerage account, but if you have a long-term goal in mind, such as retirement, you should consider something like an individual retirement account (IRA). The reason an IRA is a good way to go is that you can get tax deductions when you contribute, but the catch is that you won't be able to access the money until a certain amount of time has passed. You could also open more than one to service multiple goals.

Once you have decided on your account type, it is time to compare different brokers. You will need to have a look at things like fees, other costs, and the incentives offered. Each company will offer something different, so you should pick something that suits your needs and will reward you the most. You should also compare the convenience factor and the services on offer. The cost isn't the most important thing, especially if you are a new investor and need a little more help. Check out the features and functions you will have access to. Some brokers don't offer forex, so if that is a deal breaker for you, make sure you know what is available to you. If you want to speak to someone face-to-face, then you need to make sure that their offices are conveniently situated for you. All of these things need to be taken into account because they will impact your stock trading experience.

Now that you have done all your research, it is time to pick a brokerage firm. The best way to do this is by writing out a list of pros and cons for each firm and going through each point. You should know what your nonnegotiables are so that you can match them up to each firm. Once you have picked your firm, you can open your account there. To do this, you will need to fill out a new account application form. This is usually not a difficult process, and you will be able to do it online. Once the application is filled out, you may be asked to fill out some additional forms, but a broker can help you through the process.

Once your account has been set up, you will need to add some funds to it. There are many ways for you to do this, and your broker will be able to guide you through this. Electronic funds transfers, wire transfers, checks, and stock certificates are all options. Your broker will probably give you a minimum balance that you need to maintain in the account, so keep this in mind when you are transferring funds. Once your account is open, and you have funds in it, you can start trading. Do some research on the various stock options, make your choice, and let the process begin.

Conclusion

You should now have all the information you need to start trading in the stock market. Investing wisely is not just about knowing what the stock market is or how to trade stocks, but it is also about having the right strategy to do so. One of the best things about the stock market is that you can trade using a variety of strategies. If you have not yet figured out which one you want to try, then I would suggest going back and re-reading Chapter Two. You might find that having the full context of the book helps you choose the right strategy for you.

Once you pick your strategy, you can get going and start buying your stocks. The strategy that you pick doesn't have to be the only one that you use, so don't think that you will be stuck with it and unable to change. As time goes on, you can try out other strategies so that you can have more streams of income. It is just better to focus on one thing when you are a beginner so that you don't end up confusing yourself or taking on too much. If you find that the strategy you initially chose is not working for you, then you are free to change it up.

When it comes to the stock market, you will always be learning. There is always more information for you to take in, and this can really be a great experience. Try to use one or two of the resources that were suggested in Chapter Three. These are credible sources of information that can take your stock market knowledge to the next level. Having that extra bit of information can put you way ahead of your peers, and you will reap the rewards of that.

Whatever your financial goals, the stock market is a great place to help you reach them. It doesn't matter whether you have a lot of time or only a little time in the day to invest. There is a strategy for you. Spend some time thinking about how much time you have to dedicate to this and then commit to it. Making a commitment to yourself is one of the best ways to make sure that you actually do it. Don't let this just be a good book that you have read. Allow it to be the starting point to building the life that you have always dreamed of. You have all the information, so now all that is left to do is to use it.

References

All Star Charts. (2012, January 10). *Trading: The never-ending journey*. https://allstarcharts.com/trading-the-never-ending-journey/

Amadeo, K. (2019). *Pros and cons of investing in stocks*. The Balance. https://www.thebalance.com/stock-investing-for-the-individual-investor-3306182

Banton, C. (2020, July 16). *The meaning of whipsaw when referring to stocks*. Investopedia. https://www.investopedia.com/terms/w/whipsaw.asp

Barr, A. (2021, May 19). *The 8 best investing courses of 2021*. Investopedia. https://www.investopedia.com/best-investing-courses-4783334

Best Value Schools. (2020, July 21). *5 online resources to understand the stock market*. https://www.bestvalueschools.com/lists/5-online-resources-to-understand-the-stock-market/

Bohen, T. (2019, January 5). *40 key "stock trading terms for beginners" tips*. StocksToTrade.com. https://stockstotrade.com/40-trading-terms-beginners-infographic/

Bolander, J. (2017, March 13). *Four tips for finding out if your broker is trustworthy*. The Daily MBA. https://www.thedailymba.com/2017/03/13/four-tips-for-finding-out-if-your-broker-is-trustworthy/

BrokerChooser. (2021). *Chase you invest review 2021 - pros and cons uncovered.* https://brokerchooser.com/broker-reviews/chase-you-invest-review

Business Matters. (2021, February 15). *Pros and cons of paper trading.* https://bmmagazine.co.uk/business/pros-and-cons-of-paper-trading/

Capital Index. (n.d.). *Different types of trading strategies | trading guides.* https://www.capitalindex.com/bs/eng/pages/trading-guides/different-types-of-trading-strategies

Chen, J. (2020, September 2). *Sideways trend definition.* Investopedia. https://www.investopedia.com/terms/s/sidewaystrend.asp

Corporate Finance Institute. (n.d.). *Three best stock simulators - learn to trade stocks online.* https://corporatefinanceinstitute.com/resources/knowledge/trading-investing/three-best-stock-simulators/

Desjardins. (n.d.). *Market fluctuations: 5 things to keep in mind to stay optimistic.* Desjardins. https://blogues.desjardins.com/advicecentre/2020/04/Market-fluctuations-5-things-to-keep-in-mind-to-stay-optimistic.php

Desjardins, J. (2016, October 17). *What is a stock chart?* Visual Capitalist. https://www.visualcapitalist.com/what-is-a-stock-chart/#:~:text=It

Do It Right. (n.d.). *Understanding the tax implications of stock trading.* https://www.ally.com/do-it-right/investing/tax-implications-of-trading/

Duberstein, B. (2020, July 20). *Why patience is the most important factor in successful investing.* The Motley Fool. https://www.fool.com/investing/2020/07/20/why-patience-is-the-most-important-factor-in-succe.aspx

Dumb Bitch Trades. (n.d.). *10 Things a Trading Beginner Should Know.* https://www.dumbbitchtrades.com/beginners-trading/things-a-trading-beginner-should-know/

Farley, A. (2020a, October 1). *Pros and cons of paper trading.* Investopedia. https://www.investopedia.com/articles/active-trading/072915/pros-and-cons-paper-trading.asp

Farley, A. (2020b, November 2). *Learn how to trade the market in 5 steps.* Investopedia. https://www.investopedia.com/learn-how-to-trade-the-market-in-5-steps-4692230

Farley, A. (2021, August 31). *Market timing tips every investor should know.* Investopedia. https://www.investopedia.com/articles/active-trading/043015/market-timing-tips-rules-every-investor-should-know.asp

Fernando, J. (2019). *What margins mean in investments.* Investopedia. https://www.investopedia.com/terms/m/margin.asp

Frankel, M. (2020a, November 23). *How to open a brokerage account: A step-by-step guide.* The Motley Fool. https://www.fool.com/the-ascent/buying-stocks/how-to-open-brokerage-account/

Frankel, M. (2020b, December 23). *What is options trading?* The Motley Fool. https://www.fool.com/the-ascent/buying-stocks/what-is-options-trading/

Harper, D. R. (2019, November 19). *What drives the stock market?* Investopedia. https://www.investopedia.com/articles/basics/04/100804.asp

Hayes, A. (2020, July 13). *How does the stock market work?* Investopedia. https://www.investopedia.com/articles/investing/082614/how-stock-market-works.asp

Hayes, A. (2021a, March 13). *Short selling.* Investopedia. https://www.investopedia.com/terms/s/shortselling.asp

Hayes, A. (2021b, April 2). *Line chart definition.* Investopedia. https://www.investopedia.com/terms/l/linechart.asp

Heitkoetter, M. (2020a, January 27). *How long does it take to learn how to trade stocks.* Medium. https://markus-heitkoetter.medium.com/how-long-does-it-take-to-learn-how-to-trade-stocks-ca775c402a3

Heitkoetter, M. (2020b, October 2). *Should you start day trading? Here are the pros and cons.* FXStreet. https://www.fxstreet.com/education/should-you-start-day-trading-here-are-the-pros-and-cons-202010021708

Hill, A. (n.d.). *What are the components of a stock chart.* TradingSim. https://tradingsim.com/blog/what-are-the-components-of-a-stock-chart/

Hill, A. (2018, September 26). *8 effective ways to maintain your trading focus.* TradingSim. https://tradingsim.com/blog/trading-focus/

Invest Some Money. (n.d.). *The advantages of short selling stocks (and disadvantages!).* https://investsomemoney.com/advantages-disadvantages-short-selling-stocks/

Investopedia. (2021, April 24). *Best time(s) of day, week, and month to trade stocks.* https://www.investopedia.com/day-trading/best-time-day-week-month-trade-stocks/

Investopedia Staff. (2021, January 29). *Tax tips for the individual investor.* Investopedia. https://www.investopedia.com/taxes/individual-investor-tax-tips/

Irby, L. (2020, June 16). *10 simple ways to manage your money better.* The Balance. https://www.thebalance.com/ways-to-be-better-with-money-960664

Kennon, J. (2020, October 1). *Intro to stock trading for beginners.* The Balance. https://www.thebalance.com/stock-trading-for-beginners-357633

Kennon, J. (2021, April 19). *Basic math: Get rich with simple stock investments.* The Balance. https://www.thebalance.com/the-mathematics-of-getting-rich-by-investing-in-stocks-358105

Krishna, R. (2020, April 25). *5 common stock investing mistakes to avoid as a beginner.* Groww. https://groww.in/blog/common-stock-investing-mistakes-to-avoid-as-a-beginner/

Kuepper, J. (2021, January 28). *An introduction to day trading.* Investopedia. https://www.investopedia.com/articles/trading/05/011705.asp

LaPonsie, M. (2020, January 6). *7 steps to manage your money.* US News & World Report; U. S. News & World Report. https://money. usnews.com/money/personal-finance/articles/steps-to-manage-your-money

Majaski, C. (2020, March 25). *Paper trade: Practice trading without the risk of losing your money.* Investopedia. https://www.investopedia.com/terms/p/papertrade.asp#:~:text=A%20paper%20trade%20is%20a

Marks, W. (n.d.). *Factors that affect the stock market.* Zacks. https://finance. zacks.com/factors-affect-stock-market-2405.html

Marquit, M. (2021, May 12). *Paper trading: Practice investing with a virtual trading account.* Investor Junkie. https://investorjunkie.com/stock-brokers/virtual-trading-account/

Merritt, C. (2019, March 5). *How does a shareholder make money?* Small Business - Chron.com. https://smallbusiness.chron.com/shareholder-make-money-64589.html

Milton, A. (2020, November 18). *What is a trailing stop loss in day trading?* The Balance. https://www.thebalance.com/trailing-stop-1031394

Mitchell, C. (2020a, October 15). *Day trading tips for beginners who are just getting started.* The Balance.

https://www.thebalance.com/day-trading-tips-for-beginners-on-getting-started-4047240

Mitchell, C. (2020b, November 22). *Point-and-Figure (P&F) chart definition and tactics.* Investopedia. https://www.investopedia.com/terms/p/pointandfigurechart.asp

Mitchell, C. (2021a, February 18). *Swing trading definition and tactics.* Investopedia. https://www.investopedia.com/terms/s/swingtrading.asp

Mitchell, C. (2021b, March 25). *Understanding a candlestick chart.* Investopedia. https://www.investopedia.com/trading/candlestick-charting-what-is-it/

Mitchell, C. (2021c, May 10). *Bar chart definition and uses.* Investopedia. https://www.investopedia.com/terms/b/barchart.asp#:~:text=A%20bar%20chart%20is%20a

Muller, C. (2021, March 4). Investing 101: How to read A stock chart for beginners. *Money under 30.* https://www.moneyunder30.com/how-to-read-a-stock-chart

O'Connell, B. (2018, October 3). *How do stocks and the stock market work?* TheStreet. https://www.thestreet.com/investing/stocks/how-do-stocks-work-14726850

Rosenberg, E. (2020, April 15). *The 9 best stock market books of 2021.* The Balance. https://www.thebalance.com/best-books-for-learning-about-stocks-4171823

Rowen, L. (2020, May 14). *What exactly is the stock market?* Two Cents. https://twocents.lifehacker.com/what-exactly-is-the-stock-market-1843461592

Sebastiano, C. (2019, December 24). *Online investing: Robo-Advisors vs. online brokerages.* Ratehub.ca. https://www.ratehub.ca/blog/investing-robo-advisors-vs-online-brokerages-2/

Securities and Exchange Commission. (n.d.). *Stocks.* Investor.gov. https://www.investor.gov/introduction-investing/investing-basics/investment-products/stocks

Sharma, N.K. (2020, June 27). *Pros and cons of options trading in 2020.* Raghunandan Money. https://rmoneyindia.com/research-blog-traders/pros-and-cons-of-options-trading-in-2020/

SoFi. (2021, January 8). *A brief history of the stock market.* SoFi. https://www.sofi.com/learn/content/history-of-the-stock-market/

Study.com. (2017, September 4). *Difference between financial advisor & broker.* Study.com; Study.com. https://study.com/articles/difference_between_financial_advisor_broker.html

Sykes, T. (2019, January 3). *37 stock trading terms every trader needs to know.* Timothy Sykes. https://www.timothysykes.com/blog/trading-terms-you-need-to-know/

TED-Ed. (2019). How does the stock market work? - Oliver Elfenbaum [Youtube Video]. In *YouTube*. https://www.youtube.com/watch?v=p7HKvqRI_Bo

The Robust Trader. (2021, April 13). *What are the pros and cons of swing trading?* The Robust Trader. https://therobusttrader.com/what-are-the-pros-and-cons-of-swing-trading/#:~:text=Swing%20trading%20has%20many%20pros

TradingSim. (n.d.). *Why practice trading?* https://tradingsim.com/feature-tour/why-practice-trading/

Voigt, K. (2021a, April 23). *Robo-Advisor vs. personal financial advisor: How to decide*. NerdWallet. https://www.nerdwallet.com/article/investing/financial-advisor-vs-robo-advisor

Voigt, K. (2021b, May 23). *11 best online stock brokers for beginners of May 2021*. NerdWallet. https://www.nerdwallet.com/best/investing/online-brokers-for-beginners

Whittaker, M. (2017). *Watch out for these red flags while investing*. US News & World Report; U. S. News & World Report. https://money.usnews.com/investing/investing-101/articles/2017-10-16/watch-out-for-these-red-flags-while-investing

Williams, S. (2015, June 24). *Buying on margin: The pros and cons*. The Motley Fool. https://www.fool.com/how-to-invest/broker/2015/06/24/buying-on-margin-the-pros-and-cons.aspx

Woods, G. (2014, November 25). *5 day trader's tricks to control your emotions.* Trading Setups Review. https://www.tradingsetupsreview.com/5-day-traders-tricks-control-emotions/

www.trade-stocks-market.com. (2016, April 18). *The stock market documentary world documentary HD.* www.youtube.com. https://www.youtube.com/watch?v=Dp3IOVw-vy4

Yates, T. (2021, February 4). *4 ways to predict market performance.* Investopedia. https://www.investopedia.com/articles/07/mean_reversion_martingale.asp

Yochim, D. (2021, May 9). *Stock market simulator: How to get started with virtual trading.* NerdWallet. https://www.nerdwallet.com/article/investing/virtual-trading-stock-market-simulators

All images sourced from https://unsplash.com/

www.ingramcontent.com/pod-product-compliance
Lightning Source LLC
LaVergne TN
LVHW022221200926
848481LV00006B/2060